CONFESSIONS
OF A
CHURCH PLANTER'S
WIFE

Coming Clean about the
Dirty Side of
Church Planting

ANGIE HAMP, M.C./c.c. L.P.C.

Acknowledgments

To my handsome, talented and amazing husband, Jon, who kicked me in the pants to pursue my dreams. I am the most blessed of women, to wake up next to you every day. I love serving side-by-side with you in the trenches of church planting.

To Noah, my oldest son, your heart and love for people inspire and challenge me. I am so blessed to have you in my life, and love the way God is already using you for Him.

To Caleb, my little firecracker who never gives up, but truly lives life like Caleb in the Bible. Slay the Giants! I love your ambition and drive to conquer life and not take **no** for an answer.

What do the Hamps do? Stick together!

To my Mom, who is Jesus in the flesh. To Al and Twyla, who raised a Godly man named Jon. To Zishan, who is always there to make me laugh, and listen to me vent. To Mindy, who has always believed in me. To Robyn, who challenges me to dance through life.

To all of the church planter wives who contributed to this book and encouraged me during the writing process, I love each of you and believe in you.

Contents

Part I. The Issues No One Talks About.

1   STOP: Do Not Proceed Until You   1
    Read This Chapter

2   It's His Dream and I Want to Scream   20

3   I'm Depressed and He Couldn't Care Less   34

4   The Dangerous Game of Comparing   50

Part II. Finding Balance: Marriage, Family, Ministry and Work

5   The Other Woman--The Church   64

6   Jumping Back into the Workplace   79

7   What about My Kids?   90

8   Riding the Roller Coaster Without   101
    Tossing Your Cookies

Part III. Oh The Places You Will Go

9   You Want Me To Do What?   115

10   I Never Knew I Could Do That!   125

11   No Magic Wand or Pixie Dust   136

Part IV: Things That Make You Go Hmmmm

12 What Every Planter Wishes His Wife Knew 151
    Written by Church Planter – Jon Hamp

13 I Wish I Would Have Known That 160

Part V: Last But Not Least

14 The Importance of Relationships 176

15 Final Thoughts 181

Foreword

Just for kicks, on the day I wrote this foreword, I did a search on Amazon for "church planting." My query turned up 687 results. This was quite a contrast to my experience of trying to find a book on church planting in 1989 when I started Church on the Terrace in Utah. My Amazon search confirmed my memory. Church planting books were rare and hard to find. In fact, it appears that more church planting books have been written in the first three months of 2011 then the total available in 1989.

I'm thankful for all the great church planting books that are now available. It makes my task of equipping and encouraging church planters so much easier. It appears that the Church as a whole has gotten heaven's memo. Starting new communities of faith is not an option if we are to be with Christ on His mission. And while all these great books espouse different and even sometimes contrasting philosophies and approaches, they all agree on one thing- church planting is a hazardous endeavor, not to be taken lightly.

I agree wholeheartedly. When a leader feels called to plant a church, they are stepping right up to the frontlines of the battle and they will quickly find themselves under fire from almost every direction. Financial challenges, leadership challenges, situational obstacles, unexpected surprises and downright straightforward spiritual attack. Most of the books acknowledge these realities and give sage advice about how to deal with them.

And most of the books at least have a few paragraphs about maintaining balance between the rigors of the planting journey and being a good dad and husband.

(I'm not going to comment on the fact that most of the books assume the planter is male and married - I'll save that for another foreword!) But few (if any) have anything to say about the unique challenges of the wife of the planter.

That's why I was genuinely excited when Angie Hamp told me she was writing a book about the planting journey from the perspective of the wife of a planter. Far too many new churches are sabotaged because the planting couples overlook the impact of the planting process on the wife of the planter. And until now, the only help for wives might be found in occasional newsletters or spontaneous conversations with other planters wives.

If you are the wife of a planter, Angie Hamp has given you a gift. Her confessions are not for the faint of heart. She tells it like it is by opening up her own inner thoughts and emotions with a candor that some readers may find shocking--in a good way. If you are already on the planting journey, you will find yourself thinking, "It's great to know that I'm not the only one experiencing these challenges, thinks these thoughts and feels these feelings!" Angie's honesty in itself is a blessing. But she doesn't stop there. Using her knowledge as a professional counselor, she follows every honest disclosure with solid spiritual and mental health guidance designed to help you process the turbulence of planting in a manner that empowers you to grow through your challenges.

If you and your husband are contemplating stepping out to plant a church, reading and applying the wisdom of this book could be a marriage and ministry saver for you. Read it together and talk about how you can work together to navigate through the inevitable mine fields you will encounter. You may even choose to find some other planter wives in your neighborhood and form a book study group to maximize the benefit and find strength in numbers.

Thanks Angie for creating a much-needed resource for church planter's wives... it's not a moment too soon.

Steve Pike
Director, Church Multiplication Network
churchmultiplicationnetwork.org

Introduction

What is a *Church Planter's Wife*? The simple answer is that she is the wife of a church planter. A specific, all-encompassing definition is a whole other question, because the term *Church Planter's Wife* has many different meanings. Some church planter wives serve as co-pastors, while others prefer to be supportive and remain in the background. In the end, I do not think there is one specific definition that would adequately describe all church planters' wives.

What I do know is that church planter's wives sacrifice, work tirelessly, and encourage their husbands in the call of church planting. In addition, many planter wives work outside the home so that their husbands can focus full-time on the church plant. They give up stability, a steady paycheck; they raise children, direct ministries in the church, and rise to the challenges brought on by church planting.

Maybe there is a definition that adequately describes church planter wives. Church planter wives are heroes!

The dream for the book was born out of the tragic lack of resources available to planter wives. This book directly tackles the issues church planter's wives face in a raw and honest way. I hope that as you read my confessions, you will be uplifted, challenged and equipped in your call, and role as a church planter's wife.

I want to convey to you that I am not perfect. I do not have it all together and am flawed in many areas. I share many of the failures and shortcomings in my personal life, my marriage, my role as a mother, and as a Pastor's wife.

I desire to communicate through this book, that God has a plan for you and that church planting can be an amazing journey and experience.

Today you may question your role, your calling, even your sanity, but God is walking with you and is near to be your sustainer, provider and friend. He sees you, He is proud of you and He loves you.

As you read this book, I encourage you to grab your Bible and a journal because God desires to speak to you. He wants you to feel His presence as he dances over you.

You, my friend, are not alone in your journey as a planter wife. Prayers are offered up to Heaven daily for you. What you do matters!

Angie Hamp — Church Planter's Wife

Part I

The Issues
No One
Talks About

> 'Greater good?' I am your
> wife! I'm the greatest "good"
> you are ever gonna get!
> ~Elastigirl~

CHAPTER 1

STOP: Do Not Proceed Until You Read This Chapter

Ten Things You Must Know

When Jon (my husband) and I decided to plant a church, I believed I was ready for the challenge. After all, we had already been staff members at two other church plants, and we had 10-plus years of ministry experience under our belts. In addition, we were in complete unity and were certain that God had called us to our city to start a new church. Hand-in-hand we launched into the journey of church planting with excitement and anticipation about the incredible things God would do because of our obedience and commitment to see our city reached for Christ.

As we navigated the process of church planting, Jon and I fantasized about the church we were getting ready to launch. We envisioned many people coming to Christ and saw ourselves happy and fulfilled. We also visualized rapid growth and that the plan we had spent months praying and laboring over would be blessed by God.

Many of our dreams have come true and God has blessed us, and our church. There have also been disappointments, testing of our faith and hardships that were not a part of our original plans or dreams. I have grown and matured both as a woman and as a believer. God has used me to accomplish tasks I never knew I could, and has positioned me to be a woman of influence. In my wildest dreams, I could not have scripted this road and although there have been painful and difficult seasons; I have also experienced fulfillment and a sense of accomplishment. The road of church planting however has come at great personal cost.

Growth and maturity does not come without difficulty and trial. I don't think anyone chooses or hopes to experience adversity, but it is through trials that God's refinement comes. Whether we like it or not, God uses difficult times in our lives to get our attention and teach us utter dependence on Him. When we submit to God and His process, the fog clears in order for us to catch a glimpse of what His purpose is. Church planting accomplishes this very thing; at least it can if we let it.

There is no church planting roadmap per se, especially for wives, however I would like to offer **ten** things every church planter's wife must know to be better equipped for church planting.

Number Ten: You Will Become Elastigirl

In the movie, The Incredibles, Helen Parr a.k.a. Elasti-girl stretches around her family in order to protect them. Elastigirl's flexibility is evident as she bends and stretches to emotionally and physically adapt to the needs of her family, and the demands of her job as a su-perhero. Elastigirl not only runs her household, but she is super-wife to her stressed out husband, supervises three children, keeps a cool head in stressful situations, and rises to the challenge to protect her family in times of crisis. Oh, and she also saves the world.

Perhaps the description of Helen Parr a.k.a. Elastigirl is one you can relate to. Just like Elastigirl, you wear many hats and perform several roles as a planter wife. Juggling all of the balls required in church planting causes weariness and a feeling of being stretched in every different direction. Just when we think we have found balance or feel "in control" of our lives, something changes that requires us to adapt and change. The jour-ney of church planting is an ever-changing one that re-quires patience and flexibility.

I am sure that you have already experienced plenty of changes and the need for adaption to these changes. In the beginning, it is easy to roll with the punches, but as time progresses, we can feel "stretched" out and tired. It's in these times that patience wears thin and frustra-tion increases. In order to do more than just survive as a planter wife, it is critical that you become--Elastigirl! Flexible. Strong. Adaptable.

In church planting, flexibility is your ally and rigidity is your adversary. Many planter wives are by nature, planners and this is certainly not a negative trait; in fact it is necessary and essential. The problem is that in the world of church planting; best laid plans are often changed in the blink of an eye. This is frustrating!

Changes are inevitable, and although this goes against the grain of your planning nature, flexibility and elasticity will save your sanity.

It is also important to note that sometimes God changes plans, and we must also submit and adapt to what *He* wants to do. As humans, God gives us creativity and plans inspired by the Holy Spirit but because it is *His* church, He may choose to change the direction to better accomplish His will.

When you feel frustrated and "stretched" because you have been flexible to the point of snapping, stop and pray about what God would have you to do. Ask Him to change your heart and perspective, and to help you remember that *He* is in control and that it is *His* church. Surrendering to God, and acquiring a willingness to be "flexible" will bring back some of the elasticity, and will replace frustration with peace.

Number Nine: Your Faith Will Be Tested Like Never Before

Just the title of this section may be enough to make you want to put the book down and turn on the television. This section is not an attempt to be discouraging or give you a reality check. Instead, this portion of the book was prayerfully written so that when you feel disheartened or discouraged, you will know that what you're feeling is normal.

Many planter wives have reported that they feel like they have a huge target on their backs. They do. You do too. The enemy hates you and your husband and will try to thwart every effort you put forth to bring people to God. Sometimes, Satan attacks our faith, other times it is tested by the Lord. On the journey of church planting, it it is not only normal, but common to feel like your faith is being tested constantly.

You are in good company with heroes of the faith, and the most obvious example given to us in Scripture of a person whose faith was tested is Job. Job was tested in every possible way, but He chose to praise God anyway. In fact, Job described the testing of his faith like this, *"But he knows the way that I take; when he has tested me, I will come forth as gold."* (Job 23:10 NIV)

Job acknowledged that God tested his faith and he declared even in the midst of his suffering and pain that God would be faithful, and that much would be accomplished through difficulty.

It is easy to fall into the trap of believing that we are receiving punishment from God or that we're doing something wrong. In these times, it is tempting to look to the right or the left and wonder why God is allowing such difficulty to be brought into our lives. In times of trial, it is normal to cry out to God and question why He would allow us to experience such pain and suffering, when we obediently said yes to His call.

Questions like this are normal and acceptable to God. He does not mind when we come to Him honestly and share our feelings. God designed us as women to be emotional creatures, and He won't strike you with lightning just because you question Him. It's okay to pour out your heart out to Him. Testing of our faith is for a purpose and although there may be no good reason in your mind why He allows periods of trial, He is making you as beautiful and polished as gold. In fact, He might just be positioning you to witness a supernatural miracle.

Number Eight: You Will Witness Supernatural Miracles

Church planting opens the way for you to witness miracles, and be the recipient of miracles. If you took a moment you could probably already list many miracles God has done for you so far.

When we planted Discovery Church, our mentor Jim Ladd, encouraged us to create a file to keep a list of the miracles God did during our journey. Today, our file is full and serves as a faith builder for us. Every time I open the file, tears of joy and awe flow as I remember the incredible and supernatural miracles God has done. We have been given a car, trips, groceries, received checks in the mail to cover our mortgage, haircuts, clothes, gift cards, and the list could go on and on. In addition, our church has received support checks in the mail that covered an entire month of our lease payment and we even had a $17,000 loan forgiven. We have had the privilege of receiving many supernatural miracles!

Church planting requires utter dependence on God, but it also opens the door for Him to perform miracles that most people never get to see. When God performs miracles it is Him smiling on you and your faithfulness, and it will serve you well to remember those miracles. Write them down, or keep a file so that you can go back and recall all that God has done for you.

In Psalms 77 David cries out to God. You can almost hear the anguish in his voice until verse 10 when the whole mood of the passage changes.

David says, *"I will remember the deeds of the LORD; yes, I will remember your miracles of long ago. I will consider all your works and meditate on all your mighty deeds"* (Psalm 77:11-12 NIV).

There will be days when you will need to remember the miracles, especially during times of testing.

Number Seven: Some Days You Will Feel Insane

Once again, the title of this section is sure to make you want to throw this book out the window, but read on.

Gnarls Barkley has a song titled, "Crazy." The opening lyrics of the song say, *"I remember when, I remember, I remember when I lost my mind. There was something so pleasant about that place."* I laugh every time I hear this song and think of church planting. Because there are days that I feel like I've lost my ever loving mind.

Sometimes life is so busy and chaotic that I feel like I'm going insane. You will most likely have days you feel you are losing your mind also. Many days we as planter wives are so bogged down with tasks that it seems we use every bit of brain power available. This in turn can leave us in a fog and thus creates the sense of insanity. These feelings are normal!

One rare Sunday, I didn't have any commitments at church. Normally, I arrive two hours before service begins to help prepare for the morning service. However, I was in desperate need of a break and I just wanted to sit in service and relax, so I planned a Sunday off.

At 10:10, I received a text from my husband asking me if I was coming to church. Irritated, I informed him that I would be at church at 10:30, just like *everyone* else. His next text honestly made me believe I was going insane: "Honey church started at 10:00 and *everyone* else is already here." In that moment, I was convinced that I was indeed losing my mind. I mean, I am the Pastor's wife and I didn't even remember when service started.

I laugh now, but at the time I almost made an appointment with my doctor to see if there was something wrong with me. After talking to a friend, who gently told me to lighten up, I gained some perspective and was able laugh at myself. I realized I was not going crazy but instead was overloaded with too many tasks. I took the next day off and rested. By the end of the day, I was much more in my *right* mind.

You're going to have days you feel like you are going insane. It's normal. Let those days serve as a wakeup call that you are overwhelmed with too many tasks. Call a friend, go out for coffee or simply allow yourself to laugh a bit and realize that you are not crazy; you are a church planter's wife.

Number Six: You Will Regret Planting a Church

When I told fellow church planter's wives that I was writing a book specifically targeted to planter wives, the one resounding request I received was that the book would be honest and real. This section is about as honest and real as it gets. This "*what you must know*" tip is not an attempt to make you quit before you even get started. Instead, it is a raw account of what most of us have felt at some point in the journey.

I recently sat down with a church planter's wife who was struggling with depression. For two hours I listened to this beautiful woman explain her situation to me. She described financial hardship, stress in her marriage, dis-couragement over the growth of the church, and concern about how church planting was impacting her children. I listened with empathy and compassion as she articulated so many of the feelings and thoughts I had in my own journey. Finally, she expressed the one thought she had never verbally expressed before. She said, "*Sometimes I wish we had never planted the church.* "

Immediately after the words left her lips, she looked

horrified and started to cry. I asked her why she was crying and she poured out the guilt she felt over having such feelings of regret. From her viewpoint, it was unacceptable that she felt the way she did. After all, *"this is what God called us to do."*

The next thing I said to her changed the whole conversation. I admitted that, I too regretted planting a church at times. The look of horror on her face changed to relief as we openly shared our feelings. That conversation was life-giving and freeing for both of us, as we experienced a sense of catharsis and cleansing while stating what most church planter's wives want say, but wouldn't dare.

The conversation could have turned negative but it didn't. Simply pointing out the elephant in the room set us free and allowed us to see past the fog and reveal other feelings. Surprisingly fire and lightning didn't rain down from Heaven, either. Deep down in our hearts, we didn't really regret church planting, but we discovered it was normal to feel regret over the decision to church plant at *certain* times.

You might experience feelings of regret as well. When you do, I encourage you share them with someone you trust. When you feel the smothering emotion of regret, I hope you will remember this section and re-read it. My prayer for you during difficult seasons is that you can express your feelings to a supportive person and instead of feeling the crushing weight of guilt, you will find support and prayer.

Number Five: Temptation Will Lure You

Merriam-Webster defines temptation *as "something that*

seduces or has the quality to seduce. It is a scandalous word that most often conjures up images of people engaging in immoral acts or wicked behavior. The Bible speaks of temptation and gives many examples of people lured by temptation. When we are weak, temptation can overcome us like a boa constrictor, and clouds both our judgment, and our senses.

It has been established that church planting is difficult, and that the journey will certainly threaten your walk with Christ, as well as your marriage, your family, your finances, and even your own mental health. Often the very core of who we are is disturbed on a frequent basis leaving us weak and vulnerable to temptation. The temptation I am talking about though is not sexual or immoral temptation, but the temptation to question God's plan regarding the church plant, and seek out other ministry positions.

The truth is, during your journey of church planting, you and your husband will probably be offered multiple ministry positions. These job offers are temptations and can be very alluring, especially when you are weak.

In the town where we planted Discovery Church, there were two other church plants that launched right around the same time we did. Within a year, both churches closed, and the pastors accepted ministry positions at large churches that provided them with stability, and a nice salary. Honestly, I don't blame them, nor do I judge them. My husband talked with one of the pastors about why he chose to close his church plant after such a short time and he replied, *"It was just too hard on me and my family."* He went on to explain that he received a job offer he could not turn down.

You should always prayerfully consider doors of opportunity. God may very well call you on to a different ministry position, and there is nothing wrong with following God when He leads. As believers, we must remain vigilant though, so that we can decipher opportunity from temptation. The enemy wants your church plant to fail. He wants to destroy you and the ministry you do through church planting, therefore he will take every opportunity possible to distract you from what God has called you to do. When opportunities present themselves and you and your husband are "tempted" with alluring job offers, be careful. Take time to pray, fast, and seek the counsel of people you trust.

2 Corinthians 12:9 says, "*My grace is sufficient for you, for my power is made perfect in weakness." Therefore, I will boast all the more gladly about my weaknesses, so that Christ's power may rest on me.* (NIV).

Stay close to God and when you are weak, find your strength in Him. The saying, "*the grass is always greener on the other side*," is true and yet most of the time that grass still has many of the same issues the old grass did.

Number Four: You Will Not Recognize Yourself

The University I attended required every student to take a speech class. We had to give three speeches during the semester, which was a terrifying thought for my introverted personality type. I felt anxiety, and envisioned myself throwing up in front of the class. Somehow I made it through the speech class and managed to get a C for my grade.

That same year I fell in love with an aspiring pastor who desired to be in full-time ministry, so I knew that I would have to learn to go against my natural tendencies of being shy, and introverted to somehow be outgoing, friendly, and dare I say--*extroverted*? I struggled with this for years because my role as a Pastor's wife requires me to be someone I am naturally not.

God has been faithful, and I have slowly become someone I hardly recognize. I have gone from a shy, introverted cautious person to a confident, self-assured woman who regularly speaks in front of crowds and organizes departments, and large functions--and loves it. Sometimes I am amazed at how different I am, and credit much of this transformation to church planting. Church planting requires us to constantly step out of our comfort zones, and admittedly there are times when all of us need this challenge. Being a church planter's wife is an honor and because of the very nature of our roles as Pastor's wives, a platform is provided to influence and speak into lives. Many people climb the ladder and desire such a platform that they will never have, but God entrusts us with this responsibility.

When we submit ourselves to the work God wants to do in our lives and allow him to shape and mold us, it is incredible what He can accomplish through us. I take comfort in the wealth of examples provided in the Bible of ordinary people used to accomplish extraordinary tasks.

God desires to use you, even if you believe you are simple and *ordinary* to carry out a mission that is *extraordinary*. Through church planting, you too just might become unrecognizable—in a very amazing way!

Number Three: You Will Be Disappointed Over and Over

Disappointment is a dreaded feeling that can leave you depressed and weary. It is particularly difficult to heal from disappointments when they are frequent and when they come as we are trying with all our might to chase God and follow His call.

The reality is that disappointment is a part of life and ministry. You may have already had heartbreaking disappointments in church planting thus far that have left you feeling out of sorts and disillusioned. Perhaps you have prayed and sought God on particular issues and needs, only to have prayers unanswered.

Disappointment is a natural feeling in the journey of church planting. In my discussions with other church planter's wives, there are *three* main areas of disappointment that most planter wives deal with.

People Will Disappoint You

As believers we should love each other with the love of Christ and follow God's plan for resolving conflict. Many times we are hateful and mean to one another despite bearing the name of Jesus Christ. In your journey of church planting, people will promise you the moon and will deliver nothing. In addition, people will commit to be on your launch team only to change their minds, or decide church planting is not for them. Pastors and churches will promise you funding and support only to renege and your own denomination may fail to provide you with what they originally promised, leaving you with major disappointment.

How you handle these disappointments is very important. It hurts, and it hurts deep. Experiencing hurt and the pain of disappointment is normal, but it is also important to allow God to heal you, rather than allow resentment and bitterness to encompass your heart. God is faithful, and He will send other people who will partner with you. He will also provide the funds and finances, and open doors for your church to succeed.

Your Husband Will Disappoint You

No one stands by her man more than a planter wife. If anyone dares to mess with our husbands, we will rear up like an angry momma bear ready to defend. Our husbands have good hearts, but constantly struggle with the balance between ministry and family. Many times, ministry wins out which can leave you feeling disappointed. You may be left to wonder how you could support your husband to the degree you have, only to be neglected and unappreciated.

During the first few years of a church plant your husband will be pulled in a hundred different directions. He may neglect your marriage or your children and place the majority of his focus on the church. This is a hard pill to swallow, and no matter how many times you wave the flag of *"Hey remember me?"* he may not get it.

Be vigilant my friend, as the enemy uses such times of disappointment in marriage to wedge his way into your heart, and breed resentment and frustration. Instead, go to God with your disappointment, and ask him to open doors for you to talk to your husband. Ask God to speak to your husband and reveal to Him the need to balance ministry and marriage. Above all, keep your heart in the right place. Many times, the busyness that accompanies church planting rolls in seasons and as you gain experience as Pastors you will become better equipped to balance your marriage and ministry.

God Will Disappoint You

This is probably the worst disappointment to experience and is one most people will not admit they feel. The belief God has let us down or disappointed us is not only hard to admit, but also leaves us feeling hopeless. Most of us at one time or another have felt that our prayers hit the ceiling or fell on deaf ears. The prayers we utter are heartfelt and desperate, and yet when God does not move or provide what we need, we can be left with feelings of abandonment by our Creator.

At one point in my life, I stepped out to share some of my feelings of disappointment in God with a friend. In her own way of comforting me, she quoted the verse," *God's ways are higher than our ways,"* to me. I did not find one ounce of comfort in that verse, but instead I honestly wanted to punch a hole in the wall. God's ways are often difficult to make sense of and reconcile. I know that God has me in mind and uses times of disappointment as discipline, but I most certainly do not like it. It hurts and it pains me when God disappointments me. I feel rejected and abandoned by the One who promised to love me.

Be honest with God about your feelings of disappointment. Tell Him you are mad or that you feel hurt by Him. During times where you feel disappointed by God, go to Him, and pour your heart out to Him. He may not move immediately or send down rain from Heaven to wash away all of your problems, but He will bring comfort and peace to you.

Number Two: You MUST Develop a Network of Support

This is without a doubt one of the most crucial pieces needed in the life of a church planter's wife. Many church planters dive into the world of church planting as lone rangers. This is probably not the intention, but because the funds are typically not available in the early years to hire staff, many planters and wives find themselves isolated and alone. As a result, loneliness and a sense of *"I'm the only one who feels this way"* can ensue. In order to avoid such feelings, you must develop a network of support.

You will most likely have to step out and create this type of support system on your own. You will be tempted to put it off or if you are introverted, you may shy away from developing relationships with other pastor's wives. **DO NOT** neglect this very important component of church planting!

Here are some practical ways you can develop a support system.

Take Advantage of Church Planter's Training Events

Most church planters attend a training event or boot camp in the early stages of planting. Some organizations require spouses to attend these events, but some do not. I highly recommend that you attend such events for your own benefit, because relationships naturally form due to the nature of the format. Planters and their spouses are paired with other planters at round tables, which then creates an environment for relationships to be fostered.

Take advantage of these opportunities. Exchange e-mail addresses and phone numbers, become facebook friends. Do not be afraid to ask questions of other church planter's wives at these events! You may feel apprehensive about some of your fears or feelings, but I guarantee that the other wives are probably feeling the same way, so step out and be intentional to form relationships with other wives. The encouragement and wisdom you can provide one another is extremely valuable.

Yes I Love Technology

The development of technology has afforded multiple opportunities to connect people no matter where they live. Take advantage of technology and use it to develop and maintain relationships with other church planter wives.

Facebook is a great tool that facilitates connection between planter wives. Simply writing on another woman's facebook wall, or sending her a message that lets her know you are praying for her can make all the difference. You can even create a facebook group with other wives where you can discuss relevant topics.

Another piece of technology that provides face-to-face interaction is video conferencing software. Most of this software is free or low-cost and since many computers have built in cameras, you can be set up to talk to someone face-to-face who lives across the country in no time.

Create a group, monthly and talk with other church planter's wives about issues relevant to church planting, marriage, and raising children. The possibilities are endless. The interaction will be food for your soul and will leave you feeling encouraged and ready to tackle another day.

Find Women in Your Geographical Area

You are probably not the only church planter's wife in your area. Be diligent to find other wives in your city or area to connect with. Be bold and step out to invite other church planter's wives to coffee or lunch. It doesn't matter if she is not a part of your denomination or affiliation, as you are probably both experiencing the same issues and struggles.

The need for relationships is critical and will serve you well. Simply knowing you are not alone and that other planter wives struggle with similar issues is both encouraging and fuel in your tank to keep going.

Number One: What You Do Matters!

I love talking with church planter's wives and over the years have had the privilege of conversations where together we swapped war stories, shared ideas, encouraged each other, and spurred one other on in the journey of church planting. Church planter wives are my heroes.

I've reflected on the conversations I have had with these women and I believe that one blaring question in the back of every church planter's wife is **"DO I MATTER?"**

If I had the means to, I would rent a billboard in every city where a Church Planter's wife resides in that would read, **"WHAT YOU DO MATTERS!"** This question may seem self-serving and yet as humans we have a need to know that the work we do makes a difference. Sometimes a simple acknowledgement can motivate and encourage us to get back on the horse and keep riding, especially when we feel defeated or forgotten.

Today you are not forgotten! God sees your sacrifice, your heart, the love you have for people and the ways you serve Him. He sees your empty pantry, your small bank account, your broken down car, your tattered clothes and He wants you to know that **WHAT YOU DO MATTERS**. God is proud of you.

My sisters in Christ please know today that **YOU matter**. You are not alone, nor are you forgotten. What you do week in and week out matters, so press on my friend. People will stand in Heaven because of you. What you do matters!

The Best and The Worst

Church planting will bring out both the best and the worst in you. You will have days you fly high and feel like you can take on the world. You will also have days where you are lower than low and wonder why you ever said yes to the call of church planting. No matter what you are feeling or what you are going through, God stands ready to encircle you with His love, peace, and never ending grace. He sees you, and is aware of your situation.

There are many things you must know as you walk the road of church planting, but perhaps the most important one is to stay near to God. He will be your shelter in the storm, your faithful friend and a help in times of need.

> Women marry men hoping
> they will change. Men marry
> women hoping they will not.
> So, each is inevitably
> disappointed.
> ~Albert Einstein~

CHAPTER 2

It's His Dream, But I Wanna Scream

When church planting is NOT something you want to do.

Jon and I met at Bible College, got married, and were certain of our call to ministry. Although we were in agreement that ministry was our future, we were not in agreement about what that ministry should look like. This lack of unity caused many problems in our young marriage, and the impact of the disunity caused bumps in the road for several years. God did however work in powerful ways through this trial and grew both of us in ways we never dreamed He could.

Jon and I came from vastly different backgrounds. He grew up in Salt Lake City, Utah, and I grew up in Hereford, Texas. He was a city boy who braved living in the South for four years to complete his education, but his ultimate dream was to return to Utah and minister in a part of the country that is predominantly Mormon.

I grew up in a small town in Texas and braved living 400 miles from home to complete my education. My dream was to stay in the *great* state of Texas and go on to complete my Masters degree at Southwestern Assemblies of God University. I desired for Jon to find a ministry position in Texas so we could stay and have the best of both worlds.

Obviously, these two dreams did not align and after much debate we decided to seek God. Little did we know the answers we received from God were so vastly different that one of us would be forced to "give in" to the other one's dream for the future.

Shortly after our graduation from college, Jon's parents took us on a trip to Disneyworld. One night, Jon and his dad, Al went for a walk. Al shared with him about a new church plant they were considering becoming a part of in Riverton, Utah. Jon's Dad informed him he had spoken to the pastor about us, and that the pastor was very interested in talking with Jon and me about being a vital part of the church plant.

Jon returned to our hotel room to inform me that he had heard from God about what our future would hold. I sat up on the bed, all ears, eager to hear about the exciting adventure God had called us to—in *Texas*.

The next few minutes turned from excitement to utter disappointment as Jon outlined how God had called us to Utah to be a part of a new church plant.

He also informed me that he planned to call the Pastor upon our return from vacation to discuss the details. I said very little that night, thinking that the whole idea would lose steam, and we would return to our search of a ministry position in good ole' Texas where I could stay comfortable and pursue my Master's degree.

We returned to Texas after our vacation and early the next morning Jon got on the phone with the pastor in Utah. I left for work and pretty much blew off the idea that we would ever move to Utah. Little did I know that upon my return home that evening from work my husband intended to share his plan to move us to *Utah*.

That evening, we sat down to dinner and Jon told me that he truly believed God was calling us to Riverton, Utah. I bit my tongue hard as I tried to listen to the details with an open mind. The move to Utah would require us to pay our own expenses, secure jobs, find an apartment, and the pay would be a bit fat zero! What girl would not be swept off her feet by this amazing offer? Jon also informed me that we would be flying out to Utah the next weekend to meet the pastor and plan the move.

I don't remember much else about that night except that there was a lot of weeping and gnashing of teeth. I felt so angry and frustrated that Jon had made up his mind about Utah with very little thought regarding my dreams for the future. I was terrified about leaving Texas, my family and everything I had known my entire life. We talked in circles that night and the next several nights about the same issues. What about jobs? Where would we live? What about my goal to pursue my Master's degree at Southwestern?

Jon answered each question with patience for the first few days, but over time his patience grew thin as I asked the same questions over and over. His answers just never satisfied me because ultimately I wanted him to forget the whole crazy plan. Instead, he became more determined to pursue Utah and became hard hearted to my pleas.

The next weekend we travelled to Utah. We were greeted at the airport by Jon's parents who were excited about the prospect of their son and daughter-in-law moving to Utah to be a part of the church plant they had just committed to help launch. The next few days were a whirlwind as we met the young pastor and his wife, looked for jobs, viewed apartments, and attended the Saturday night service at the new church to meet the congregation. There were seven people there, *including* us.

Miraculously, in the course of three days we both secured jobs and found a beautiful apartment. We had dinner with the pastor and his wife on our last night in Utah and everyone at the table discussed how God had supernaturally opened the doors for us to come to Utah. I remember sitting at the table, sick at my stomach and did not agree with this consensus. I thought that perhaps *Satan* had opened all of the doors and that this move was going to spell disaster. I kept my thoughts to myself.

We returned to Texas to prepare for our move to Utah. Those days were filled with many tears as I packed up my beautiful little house in the country and got ready to bid farewell to family, friends, and--*my dreams*.

Whereas I spent my last days in Texas angry, sad and scared, Jon on the other hand, was full of excitement and anticipation. At farewell dinners with friends he repeatedly told people about how God was fulfilling **his** dreams to return to Utah and minister. He went on to explain how he so often daydreamed about planting a church in Utah where he grew up, and how God had answered *his* prayers to be a part of such a work.

As I had done so often over the last few weeks, I bit my tongue and fought back the tears. Inside I screamed, "What about my dreams?" "What about what I want to do?" **"I DON'T WANT TO GO TO UTAH!!"**

The drive from Texas to Utah was a trail of tears for me. A strong sense of doom set in and fear gripped my mind and heart as the "Welcome to Utah" sign stared me in the face. My husband, who pulled a truck with a U-Haul trailer called me on my cell phone as I drove the car behind him, and proclaimed that our future was going to be great, and that God had amazing things in store for us in *Utah*.

Honestly, our first few weeks in Utah were not all that bad. I settled into life and tried my best to make a home in a city that was completely foreign to *me*, yet home to *Jon*. The small church plant we attended and worked at had around 15 people and they were very nice, and excited to have us join them to reach Salt Lake City. In addition, the Pastor and his wife were gracious and kind to us, and frequently affirmed our call to Utah. I started my new job as an intake counselor at a local Employee Assistance Program and began to make some friends at my workplace. The people in Utah were also kind and seemed to welcome a Texan to their state. Unfortunately, the feelings of anger, resentment, and fear that I had pushed down for weeks reared their ugly heads on many occasions.

The Ugly Truth

Over the next few months, I became a person I hardly recognized. Several times a week, I had horrible angry outbursts directed right at Jon. Several of my friends had entered graduate programs and full-time ministry positions that seemed quite glamorous compared to the tiny church we were at. The cost of living was much higher in Utah which required Jon to work a second job so we could make ends meet. I found myself very lonely as I sat at home many nights while my husband worked. On the weekends, Jon worked at the church and again, I sat alone trying to swim in a pond with no familiarity or sense of reason.

The distance in our marriage grew and the fighting also became very intense. Jon was extremely patient with me for the first several months but became weary of the constant crying and nagging I made him endure. Soon, his heart toward me grew hard and he too became angry and resentful. I sunk deep into depression, (which I discuss in detail in Chapter Three) and Jon became even more frustrated with my lack of ability to *"just deal with it,"* and be happy. On multiple occasions, family members and friends told me that I was going to ruin his ministry if I did not *"get my act together."* This most certainly did not help me and again the ugly three-headed monster of **anger, resentment,** and **fear** reared its head. It served to torture me day after day until bitterness and hate embedded itself so deep in my heart, I was a shell of whom I once was.

The distance and fighting in our marriage continued until the chasm in our relationship was so deep that we began to discuss divorce. Both of us felt lost and alone. We were roommates and were on completely different levels in every area of our lives. The ugly truth is that we both made some terrible decisions that had far-reaching consequences in our individual lives and in our marriage. The obstacles seemed too great and too big and we were both exhausted from months of struggling.

A Bit of a Breakthrough

Jon admitted that life in Utah was not at all that he envisioned. Utah is tough ground for church planting and although the church had grown to some extent, it took patience and diligence to keep the faith and continue. Jon also acknowledged that he was frustrated that he was doing very little ministry and instead poured the majority of his time into a job he had no passion for, just for us to survive financially. This conversation served as a bit of a breakthrough for us because as women when our husbands are humble, it typically softens our hearts toward them.

I also had plenty to admit as I had let anger, resentment, and fear rule my life. It changed me into a horrible, ugly person, and it was no wonder my husband had very little compassion for me. I constantly attacked him and disrespected him on every level. Honestly, I had emasculated my husband for months, and hurled insults that threatened to destroy his self-image. I hated myself and who I had become. The depression I was in was like a 12-foot anaconda wrapped around me so tightly that I could not breathe. It sucked the life out of me.

Along with that, the enemy often whispered in my ear and admittedly I listened to his voice, rather than the voice of God. Ironically, I spent my days listening to other people's problems as a counselor, and yet I could not seem to help myself navigate the issues in my life or in my marriage. I felt like a failure and spent most days in a pattern of self-loathing until finally, I sought out help. Slowly, things began to turn around.

A Positive Sign

Almost a full year passed since our move to Utah. Jon and I made some strides in our marriage and the talk of divorce stopped. We continued to work on our marriage and went to a Christian counselor. Within a few weeks of starting counseling our love for one another flourished in a new, mature way. Jon vowed he would never again move us anywhere unless we were in complete agreement, which served to further soften my heart toward him. My husband was humble during this restoration period as was I. Those weeks were full of God's grace and mercy toward us to which I am still to this day, so grateful for. God took what the enemy intended for evil and turned it around for *His* good.

God continued to be faithful in the healing process and as we grew closer to one another, we began to desire a baby. There are babies everywhere in Utah, and most women my age already had one or two children, and so it is easy to catch baby fever. We had tried for a year to conceive, until one day it dawned on me that my cycle was a couple of weeks late. I did a pregnancy test and lo and behold it was positive! The plus sign on the test was a blessing and affirmation that God's hand was on our lives. I fell to my bathroom floor and thanked God for His grace and mercy. The final hold the three-headed monster of anger, resentment, and fear had on me released me from its clutches that day.

I once believed God abandoned me, but as I clutched a positive pregnancy test, I emerged from the bathroom ready to embrace healing and life, as a new life grew inside me. I called Jon and told him the news to which he responded with excitement and anticipation. We continued marriage counseling, and as I released the embedded feelings of bitterness I found joy and a love for--Utah! Who knew God could turn my hate for the State of Utah into a love and burden to see people come to know him? I started to engage in relationships with people at the church plant, and became a true part of Jordan Valley Worship Center. In doing so, I discovered such joy and healing through ministry in *Utah*.

Things were looking up as we finally found the **unity** that eluded us, when the whole crazy journey began. Unity served to strengthen us and prepare us for a test that came out of the blue.

A Test: Or a Release from Utah?

Jon and I were plugging along and doing quite well when he received a call from a Pastor, who wanted to discuss the possibility of hiring Jon to be a full-time youth pastor. The church was in Colorado, (where I had always wanted to live) and seemed to be our ticket out of Utah. We were both excited about the option to move and serve full-time in ministry, so we agreed to visit the church and interview with the pastor. The trip was wonderful, and the church was very receptive and kind to us. At the end of the weekend, the Pastor offered us the position and it seemed that God had opened the doors for us to exit Utah, and enter a new phase of our lives in-- *Colorado*. Both Jon and I felt a check, although neither one of us communicated this to the other. We agreed to pray about the job offer and went home to Utah to mull over our options.

Strangely, as we crossed the state line and I read, *Welcome to Utah*, sign again; I could not help but take note of how different I felt versus the last time I read that sign. I had this bizarre sadness and longing to remain in Utah.

I wrestled with these feelings and was frustrated at myself because I could not just accept this free pass out of Utah. Jon remained true to his word that we would not accept any new ministry position unless there was unity and complete agreement. We discussed the pros and cons and how great it would be to serve in full-time in ministry. I was in my first trimester of pregnancy and Jon accepting this position would allow me to stay home with our baby. Everything seemed perfect about the job and yet again the nagging sense of sadness and longing to stay in Utah enveloped me. The stubborn side of me kicked in and I stayed silent for hours about my struggle. I felt as if I had a devil on one shoulder and an angel on another as two conflicting voices filled my head. Suddenly, the Holy Spirit spoke and broke through with such clarity that I could not ignore. He told me that God had great things in store for us--in *Utah*.

I guess The Holy Spirit was speaking to Jon simultaneously because almost at the same instant, we looked at each other and declared that we should stay in Utah. With this obedience came such peace, such joy, and anticipation I had never experienced before. The conversation soon moved from moving to Colorado, to plans and dreams about what God would have us to accomplish in Utah. Talk a complete 180!

God Kept His Promise

Six months later I gave birth to our first son and we named him Noah Jonathan. His name means, "*a gift from God who will bring peace.*" Noah brought such joy to our lives on the day he was born and I felt God in the delivery room that day whisper that He was proud of me and my obedience to Him. God's grace and mercy is astounding and incomprehensible, and I am thankful He shows us grace and mercy even when we are so undeserving.

Two months after Noah was born God again blessed us and we bought our first home in a town just outside of Salt Lake City. The neighborhood where we moved was in a young community full of Mormon families with small children. Soon after our move, the church began to pay Jon part-time, which let him to quit one of his jobs. God allowed me to keep my job but miraculously opened the door to do my job from home. We were so happy and fulfilled. God filled our storehouses and soon the church grew to the point where they brought Jon on full-time.

God opened doors no man could ever open for us to minister on multiple occasions to our neighbors. We loved our neighborhood and became friends with our Mormon neighbors. Many of them had heard myths of Pastors, which we found humorous but nonetheless they often came to us for counsel and prayer in times of difficulty.

God also blessed our ministry at Jordan Valley Worship Center and used us in every way imaginable. Our Pastors, Stan and Olivia Nelson mentored Jon and I during our tenure in Utah and allowed us to grow and mature. They were patient, loving, supportive, and we credit them with instilling in us a passion for church planting. We learned valuable lessons in Utah and little did I know how much this would prepare us for the future.

A year later I began a Master's degree in Counseling through University of Phoenix. God didn't forget my dream to complete my Master's degree and provided a degree program that allowed me to raise my infant son, work my job, and attend school. God's plan is always perfect!

A few months after beginning school, I discovered I was pregnant again, and soon we welcomed a second son named Caleb Jonathan into our lives. The name Caleb means *"faithful"* and his name was fitting, since our God had indeed been *"faithful"* to us.

Just two weeks after Caleb was born, we received another call from a Pastor in Colorado Springs, who was starting a new church and wanted us to be a part of the church plant as Youth Pastors. Jon kindly told the Pastor we were happy where we were at, but the Pastor asked us to pray about the opportunity. We did pray about moving to Colorado Springs and felt like God wanted us to visit Colorado Springs and interview with the Pastor. The next weekend, we trekked across snowy I-70 with a newborn and through the course of the weekend; the Holy Spirit was clear in his direction that we were to move to Colorado.

I was sad as we told our church goodbye and prepared to move to Colorado. Our neighbors in Utah were also sad and many of them told us that we *"were a light in the neighborhood."* As we drove away from our townhome in Utah, both Jon and I wept. God had done such miracles in our lives, and we had grown and matured in many ways. We moved to Utah and quickly became two very broken people who wanted to leave the ministry and our marriage; however, four years later we left Utah happy, fulfilled, and ready for our next ministry assignment.

When I read the sign titled, *"Leaving Utah,"* I cried tears of sadness and joy. Once again, I reflected on how different I was and how much God had done in my life. I looked at my two young boys who slept in their car seats and shook my head in amazement at God's blessings. I prayed to my God, my Redeemer that I would never again let the three-headed monster of anger, resentment, and fear ensnare me or keep me from a life with Jesus.

Right or Wrong

When I share my story with people, they ask how we navigated out of disunity to find unity, right where we were. Many women have accused me of "*giving in*" and have bitterly told me that Jon should have moved where I wanted to go after what *"he did to me."* I do not feel anger about these questions or perspectives, as I understand why they are asked and given.

The best answer I can give is that there comes a point when you have to lay down your right to be right. Jon and I were both **right,** and we were both **wrong.** God used our situation to teach us two huge lessons: **submission** and **obedience.** Simply moving to another place was not going to solve the issues. The grass is greener on the other side, mentality will always steer you to look for even greener grass. It is a myth and the more we try to run from submission and obedience to Christ, the more likely it is that we will continue in our misery.

I sat in my misery for a full year and my only regret is that I would have just submitted to Christ and obeyed Him sooner. Jon feels the same way.

Jon and I both made huge mistakes that had far-reaching consequences that shook both of us to the very core and foundation. For months we struggled with shame over the mistakes we made however, God is not a God of shame and has used our story several times to minister to others.

I hope the honesty of this story has somehow touched you. Perhaps you related to the feelings and struggles I shared. Maybe you and your husband are presently not in unity and you find yourself in a ministry position you never wanted or desired. I wonder if the three-headed monster of anger, resentment, and fear has ensnared you? God's heart is to see you and your husband find healing and freedom, and my heartfelt prayer is that you find wholeness in Christ, and that He opens doors that lead you to Him. God stands ready to restore and redeem you even if it's his dream and you want to scream.

Today, I pray that you will bow your heart toward the King, even if you and your husband are not in unity about church planting. It doesn't matter who is right, or who is wrong. It is ultimately about the condition of our heart. If we get that right—we will never go wrong.

> Depression is nourished by
> a lifetime of ungrieved and
> unforgiven hurts.
> ~Penelope Sweet~

CHAPTER 3

I'm Depressed and He Couldn't Care Less

He's happy. You're depressed. How can you both feel so differently?

"Can I talk to you?" I stopped the conversation I was engaged in and turned around to see a young woman who looked desperate and scared. "Of course," I said. I steered us away from the crowd of people to a quiet corner, so we could talk in private.

Tentatively, the young woman poured out her heart to me and shared about how weary she was. She went on to explain that her husband was happier and more fulfilled than he had ever been and that despite how much she tried, she just couldn't seem to muster up any excitement for church planting.

I listened with compassion and empathy as the woman said, "I think I'm depressed. Could you please pray with me?"

I had just shared my own story of depression at a workshop this young woman attended. I talk about my story a lot, even though it is difficult because after all these years, my struggle with depression still brings up some residual feelings of shame.

I could tell this woman also felt shame as she shared her own struggle with depression. It made me wonder how many other church planter wives suffer in silence because they're ashamed.

We prayed together and the woman expressed some relief over having just talked about the depression. As she walked away, I sat alone feeling burdened about how many other church planters' wives I had spoken to over the years, who after hearing my story shared their own issue with depression.

The conclusion I came to that night, and now is that depression is a very real issue among church planter's wives. That's why I'm speaking out—in black and white to share my story with you. My hope is that you will know you are not alone and that there is hope.

How Does A Person Become Depressed?

There are myths about depression and an all around stigma about depressed people. Depression is a word that strikes fear and conjures up images of people in strait jackets who rock back and forth in corners at creepy mental hospitals. As a therapist, I can assure you that this is not the typical form depression takes in people.

According to webmd.com,[1] there are nine major causes

---

[1] http://webmed.com/depression/guide/causes-depression

of depression. They are **abuse, medication, conflict, death or loss, genetics, major life changes, illness, personal problems,** and **substance abuse**. It is possible to experience a combination of these causes at one time, which in turn can be a perfect *cocktail* for depression.

Church Planting Is a Cocktail for Depression

The potential for a so called "cocktail for depression," is high in church planting. Because church planters and their wives encounter many of the main causes of depression, both are at a high risk for developing clinical depression. There have been no formal studies conducted regarding the rate of depression among church planter's wives but many are struggling with depression at an alarming rate.

One major consideration not often discussed is the conflict that exists between a planter and his wife, when the planter is fulfilled, and the wife feels the complete opposite. Sadly enough, Pastors and their wives are not exempt from the clash of differences that come into play when two people feel completely *different* about the *same* issue. Perhaps you are currently in this clash of differences where your husband is thrilled and excited about church planting but you feel sad and depressed. How can you both feel so differently?

This chapter will provide more detail about my own journey through depression and will also offer hope about how to overcome the darkness of depression, and find wholeness and healing.

A Whole Lot of Baggage

Our move to Utah to help plant a church came with a whole lot of baggage. Not only were we in disagreement about the move, but we also quickly drifted apart in the first few months of our tenure at the church. I was very lonely as a young 23-year-old who felt I was in a foreign country with no friends and very little support.

I had three of the main causes of depression which were **personal problems, conflict, and major life changes**. These three causes of depression stared me in the face, and made me a prime candidate for depression.

Four weeks after we moved to Utah, I developed a hideous eye infection. I felt like I had a piece of glass in my eye and sought out an ophthalmologist to help me. As he examined my eye, he began to question me about possible causes of the infection. He asked me one question that started the waterworks in such way that the poor doctor probably thought I had lost my mind. He asked me if I cried a lot. The answer was yes, and I proceeded to explain to him about how my husband forced me to move to Utah, and that I could not stop crying. The doctor had quite the bedside manner and quickly informed me that I better find a way to stop crying so much so that I could get rid of the infection. Easier said than done!

I left his office feeling more hopeless and alone than ever. The analytical side of me knew I needed to pull myself together as I reasoned all the factors that made my life in Utah, "not that bad." The emotional part of me just could not seem to comprehend what the analytical side of me was asking, and I sank deeper and deeper into depression.

All I wanted to do was feed the depression and sought out every opportunity to do so. I held on to resentment and anger, isolated myself from other people, did not eat properly and slept anytime I could. Ironically

I worked at a counseling office and spent the better part of my days *helping* people with their problems, yet I could not seem to *help* myself.

I had never before experienced such pain and darkness. I felt as if I was in a tunnel and the darkness of depression smothered me at every turn. I woke up depressed; I experienced depression throughout the day and went to bed with the same darkness. Depression was my constant companion.

Shame on You!

Another overwhelming sense that accompanied my depression was the shame I felt. It did not help that well meaning people in my life made comments and expressed frustration over my inability to deal with life in Utah. The comments and disappointments expressed by others further served to feed the monster of depression, and my own shame.

The thought of getting help did cross my mind on a frequent basis, I was the ultimate hypocrite as I spent my days helping other people with their problems, and praised them on their willingness to get help, yet I was not so eager to seek out help for myself. Somehow I could not overcome the stigma of depression in my own life, nor could I conquer the sense that as a Pastor's wife *and* a counselor, I should have it together. The months wore on and I continued to *function* in depression; if you could call it functioning. I had very little motivation to get better and instead constantly dwelt on the unfairness of my situation.

He Just Doesn't Understand

My husband Jon is a very caring individual who loves deeply but during my journey of depression, I certainly did not feel his love or that he had a clue about what I was going through. There was a huge chasm in our perspective and viewpoint of the situation. He viewed our ministry as fulfilling; fun and a dream come true. I saw our situation as a sentence, and that we were paying penance for something. Two vastly different perspectives widened the gap in our marriage and Jon became hard heartened against me after several months.

I have talked with many planter wives who report similar situations. It is not that any of our husbands choose to be unsympathetic to our feelings but sometimes men have difficulty relating to us as women. God made men and women completely different and sometimes these differences cause distance.

Men typically compartmentalize situations and view them in an unemotional way. Women on the other hand, view most situations from an emotional viewpoint and chain events together. A man who tries to help his wife with depression may say something like this to her, "*well, I'm sorry you feel this way, but let's get over it and move on.*" A wife in this situation is desperate for his understanding and listening ear and does not simply want a "solution." She desires to be heard, understood, and partnered with to overcome the depression.

Many times, as in my situation an outside perspective, such as a professional counselor can provide this insight to a husband. While getting to that point is very difficult, it can be done.

A Kick in the Pants

Eventually, I sought out professional help and my

therapist helped me identify some motivating factors that helped to jumpstart my process of overcoming depression. I discovered two key motivators that kept me going in the process of counseling. First, I was just sick and tired of being depressed. Second, I missed my marriage and desired the friendship with my husband to return.

Motivation is a key component to overcoming depression. In my practice as a therapist, when I provide an assessment for depression, I seek to determine if there is any kind of motivation the person has to help kick start the process.

Sometimes women feel very little motivation, as I did, and yet any small piece of motivation can make the difference between stagnation and progress. If you are currently struggling with depression, take a moment to discover what your motivation is to overcome depression. This will at least provide some rope for you as you seek to climb out of depression.

The Big Question: How Do I Get Out of Depression?

So just how does a person climb out of depression? The answer, and the journey are not easy but I ensure you it can be done. Identifying some of the main causes of depression is key in helping you understand some of the reasons you became depressed.

In my case, as noted earlier there were three main reasons I became depressed. First, there was **conflict** in my marriage, and within myself. This conflict seemed to have no resolution as Jon and I remained on opposite sides of the fence. Second, I had **personal problems**. I was ashamed of my depression, and had major issues in my marriage. Third, I had experienced some major **changes** in my life. I graduated from college, moved across the country, was newly married, and had a new job. Some of these changes were good changes, and yet research shows that even good changes in our lives can trigger depression.

My therapist helped me to understand how these factors played a role in my depression. She also helped me see that I had endured loss over leaving friends and family and that my dream to continue in Graduate school did not happen. I also discovered in the process of counseling that my father struggled with depression, so genetics also potentially played a role. In the end, we came to the conclusion that I had **five** out of the **nine** causes of depression. No wonder I was depressed!

In addition to individual counseling, Jon and I received marriage counseling and as healing in our individual lives and our marriage happened, the depression began to finally lift. The therapist helped Jon to understand a bit more about why I felt the way I did. She also provided insight for me to understand my husband's point of view.

I will never forget the morning I woke up and did not feel the crushing weight of depression. I literally jumped on my bed and thanked God for freeing me from the chains of depression. What a feeling!

God Is Faithful

As I healed, I began to pray that God would open doors of opportunity to minister to other women who struggle with depression. God answered that prayer then, and continues to do so now. I have spoken many times on the issue of depression and have devoted a large portion of my practice to work with women. I enjoy the work I do with women around this issue, and God has been faithful to use me to walk with women through the darkness of depression. Working with women struggling with depression is an honor because of my own journey through depression, and I have witnessed firsthand miracles as many ladies, pastors wives included have found freedom.

No matter how deep in depression you are, there is hope and there is a path to light and wholeness. Sometimes what we wish for more than anything is a roadmap with practical points so that we can navigate difficulties. The next section provides such a roadmap that offers some sensible and realistic steps you can take to climb out of depression.

A Roadmap Out of Depression

Find a competent Christian counselor. This can be very difficult but is a major key to get out of depression. Perhaps you have no clue where to find such a counselor. One suggestion is to ask a friend or two for a recommendation. If you do not feel comfortable asking a friend for a referral, there are ministries that assist with referrals to Christian counselors.

Focus on the Family is an excellent resource for assistance in finding a therapist and the process for getting a recommendation from Focus on the Family is simple. You can visit their website at: www.family.org, or call at 1 800 –A-FAMILY.

If neither of these options works, it is up you to seek out a therapist in your area. Counseling can seem scary, and the feelings of fear and apprehension are normal, but go to the first session and try it. If after the first session, you do not connect with the therapist, try another one. Do not stop until you find a competent Christian counselor to walk with you.

See A Doctor. Many people do not know that medical issues can often cause depression. Some of the leading medical concerns that cause symptoms of depression are heart disease, thyroid issues, hormonal imbalance, and hypoglycemia. Go to your doctor for a complete physical. It is important to rule out any medical issues that could either be causing the depression or exasperating the depression.

Deal with Unresolved Anger. Unresolved anger is toxic and if not dealt with can lead to depression. Identify the causes of your anger and seek ways to forgive the people you are angry with. During this process the need for a competent counselor is crucial as he or she can walk with you and guide through this process. If you do not have a counselor, find a trusted friend who you can be open and honest with.

Find ways to get outside of yourself. When we are depressed our natural tendency is to turn inward and isolate ourselves. We become numb to the world around us and forget that others are in pain or need encouragement. As crummy as you might feel, force yourself to reach out to someone else in need. Maybe you have a friend going through a difficult season; if so write her a nice card or e-mail. Perhaps someone in your church recently had a baby or is ill; make them a nice meal and take it to their home. Actively doing small acts of kindness is like a healing balm to the soul. You will feel better about yourself and in turn will minister to someone else in need. This step is certainly not easy, but is crucial in the roadmap to overcoming depression.

Develop and implement a self care plan. Many women do not properly care for themselves. We are nurturers and so we often care for everyone else around us, but neglect ourselves. If you don't take care of yourself, you will become depressed or remain in depression.

Here is a five-step self care plan that I give my clients and also use myself. The clients I have who implement this plan see results in just a few days. I call this plan the **"Daily Five."**

The Daily Five

Eat Healthy – Slamming a handful of Doritos for lunch is not healthy. When we don't eat healthy, our blood sugar drops and we feel lethargic and--*depressed*. I do not need to give you a meal plan or some type of special diet to follow. In our society, we have been educated enough to know what we should and should not eat. Fill your diet with healthy foods. Cut down on caffeine and sugar and drink plenty of water. God designed your body and gave you common sense enough to know what you should eat, so do it. Proper nutrition will help lift the depression.

Get Enough Rest – Notice I said *enough* rest. Women, who are depressed either, sleep too little or too much. Try to get at least six hours of sleep at night. If you have trouble sleeping, develop a bedtime routine. Take a bath, drink chamomile tea, turn off the television, and do not discuss anything of significance after 9 p.m. Read your Bible or pray before you go to bed and ask God for "sweet sleep." On the flip-side, you may feel like doing nothing but sleeping. Try to refrain from too much sleep as this can just fuel the depression.

Exercise and Sunshine – Your body needs some type of physical activity daily. I am not advocating that you become a pro-athlete. A 20-minute walk four or five times a week should suffice, and if you are able to, exercise outdoors. The sunshine is food for your body and the natural vitamin D the sun provides does wonders to help regulate the chemicals in your brain. Regular exercise and sunshine also helps with stress and sleep issues.

Do Something For Yourself – Once again, the natural tendency women have to nurture and care for others will serve as an obstacle for making this fourth tip happen. Do not let it! Women are notorious for neglecting themselves and many times are the last on the list, but doing things for ourselves provides fuel for our empty tanks. When we neglect this piece of self care, depression can be the result.

For most of us getting a pedicure or a massage is not something we can do daily and yet it is easy to find small ways to spoil you.

Here are some suggestions: take a hot bubble bath, make your favorite snack, read a chapter of a book, paint your nails, watch your favorite television show, go out with a friend, go for a walk. The suggestions are endless. The point is, find one small thing you can do just for you daily. You deserve it!

Spend Time With God – This one should go without saying, but many times this spiritual discipline is neglected, especially if you have prayed for God to lift the depression and it hasn't. You may believe God rejected you, or that your prayers are hitting the ceiling, but communication with God is important even when we *feel* disconnected from Him.

When I was depressed, I read Psalms many times. The short chapters were all I could comprehend, but I related to David and through reading Psalms realized that even David – a man after God's own heart had bouts of depression. Psalms provided short spurts of hope during very dark days. Even if it is just five or ten minutes a day, take this time to spend with God.

The Daily Five

Life After Depression

The roadmap provided may strike you as simplistic, and you may wonder how something so easy could be the "cure" for your depression. So my challenge to you is to try it for two weeks. If you do not feel less depressed and healthier after **seeing a counselor, getting a physical, dealing with unresolved anger, stepping outside yourself, and implementing a self care plan,** then send this book to back me and I will refund your money. I realize I sound like an info-merical. The point is, commit to take steps to get out of depression.

The path out of the darkness of depression is not easy and will take hard work. You are not alone in your journey, as many planter wives have found themselves in the same darkness you may currently be in.

I've been there, and although it was a gloomy and hard season in my life, I also learned a great deal about myself. Through my journey I learned about certain triggers that can cause me to quickly spiral downward. I also learned that I need to set boundaries and have realistic expectations for myself and others.

Stop for a moment and think about what God may want you to learn about yourself during your journey of depression. Perhaps there are life issues you have had for years that you have continued to bury. Depression can be a means in which to dig up root issues that need to be flushed out. Prayerfully consider the list of the nine causes of depression you may be dealing with and how you can work through the causes.

There is life after depression and God stands ready to walk with you during the darkness, to provide light and hope.

Reflection Questions

1. The nine major causes of depression are: abuse, medication, conflict, death or loss, genetics, major life changes, illness, personal problems, and substance abuse. Which of these do you relate to?

    _____

    _____

2. What are three life issues you struggle with?

    _____

    _____

3. How will you commit to implement and stick to a self care plan?

    _____

    _____

4. Pray for God to remove the shame and guilt associated with depression and instead provide peace and direction as you seek to get out of the darkness of depression. Write down what the Lord is saying.

    _____

    _____

    _____

> Men look *at* themselves
> in mirrors. Women look
> *for* themselves.
> ~Elissa Melamed~

CHAPTER 4

The Dangerous Game of Comparing

So how many people do you have in your church? How many showed up to your launch service? Does your husband get paid full-time from the church or does he work another job? How many ministries in the church do you oversee? How many people have been saved in your church?

Questions. People ask them want to know the answer. Some of the motives for wanting to know the answers to certain questions are asked out of true concern. In ministry we **ALL** compare and sometimes the questions asked are an attempt to compare notes; to see who is doing what. You may wonder what the problem is with asking these types of questions or comparing yourself against other church planters and church planter's wives. The truth is, nothing is wrong with curiosity and wanting to know genuinely about what other planters are doing.

Comparing is natural and yet the game of comparing can be dangerous and lead to restlessness, and self-loathing.

The Old Game We Play

For years my husband and I have attended Ministers conferences and leadership forums. I highly recommend the attendance of these events because they provide fellowship, and encouragement.

Truthfully though, these types of events can be a breeding ground for the dangerous game of comparing. Here is how the typical scenario at these events goes: Ministers walk into the room, stop and scan the room. Women look at what all of the other women are wearing and immediately question their choice of outfit. The thoughts of, *"I should have dressed up more, or I dressed up too much,"* go through their minds. Men scan the room to see who is talking to whom and immediately began to think of the answers to the questions listed above they know they are going to be asked. Soon, the ministry couple crosses the room to engage in conversation with fellow pastors. Pleasantries are exchanged and soon a hearty, *"good to see you brother, we've been praying for you; how's the church plant going"* question is asked.

Your husband stops and takes a deep breath. He squeezes your hand as he launches into all of the amazing things God has done through the church plant and how much more is anticipated for the coming year. The ministry couple sighs as they await the next question and inevitably -- the *comparison.*

Then here it comes. *"Well, I heard that so and so had twice the number on his launch Sunday and they're now running triple the number of people. They've also given thousands of dollars to missions, and his wife is the children's pastor and women's director. He's blowing it up in his church plant."*

The person who so eloquently provided the report of the other church planter may as well of punched you in the gut. You see your husband deflate and you too feel the shame associated with not doing as well as others. You wholeheartedly agree with the person about the incredible things God has done at the other church plant, but quickly yet politely say your goodbyes and walk away--to the next encounter where inevitably you will do the same song and dance.

By the end of the conference, you are so discouraged by the comparisons that you wonder what the point of your church plant is and contemplate quitting altogether. As a planter wife, you reflect on what all the other church planter wives are doing and conclude that you just do not do enough in the church. The stories of other planter wives who direct children's programs, women's ministries, work full-time jobs and leap tall buildings in a single bound start to get to you. Soon, your already shaky self image is further threatened.

You have just been ensnared by the dangerous game of comparing.

A Familiar Game

Let's face it; as women we *all* compare. My husband jokes that women don't dress for men, but instead they dress for other women. He noted this after attending a women's retreat I spoke at. He couldn't believe that at the retreat there were no men but the women dressed to the nines.

Women are notorious for comparing and within a few seconds of walking into a room, will sum up who is fatter, thinner, prettier, uglier, cuter, and dressed better than she is.

We have played the old game of comparison since we were little girls. In middle school, we compared ourselves to the popular girls or those who wore bras and started their periods first. In High School, we compared ourselves to the Homecoming Queen or the girl who got asked out by the hottest guy in school. In college, we compared ourselves to the sorority girls and to those who achieved Summa Cum Laude. As adult women, we compare ourselves to who has the cleanest house or who lost the weight six weeks after the birth of a child.

As planter wives, we compare the size of our church with other church plants, and evaluate how we support our husbands. We look at what roles we fill in the church and how much of a rock star we are—*compared* to other planter wives.

The result of this game of comparison leaves us feeling inadequate and all around down on ourselves. The game of comparing does not ever stop and is almost like a crazy drug that we become addicted to.

So, why the big need for comparison? Perhaps by engaging in this game, we are trying to fill needs or holes in our lives.

A Bottomless Pit

People often accuse pastors of being insecure. People also say pastors are arrogant, full of pride, and narcissistic. So which perspective is accurate? Most pastors and their wives are humble, have servant's hearts and desire to see the people they pastor strong in their faith, yet pastors often endure criticism, and downright meanness from people. Contrary to what people believe, we as pastors are not superhuman, but instead have the desire for affirmation just like everyone else. However, sometimes this affirmation we so desperately desire is sought in all of the wrong places, instead of in God. When we seek out affirmation from other people, it is like a bottomless pit that has no end.

As women, we too have the need for affirmation, but it is very important to examine this need for affirmation and discover if the desire for affirmation stems out of insecurity, and the need to "fill a hole" in our lives.

Perhaps you never received praise or compliments from your parents or there are past hurts that send you spinning into the bottomless pit of comparing.

I personally have struggled with insecurity as well as low self esteem. My father was not particularly complimentary of me. He never told me he was proud of me, nor did he tell me I was pretty. I desperately desired my dad's approval, and tried every way possible to get that approval. I was a straight-A student, won awards for playing my flute and flourished as a dancer, but my dad never attended one of my events. I remember graduating from high school and peering high into the bleachers hoping to catch a glimpse of my father, but the seat next to my Mother was empty.

When I was 18, my Dad passed away unexpectedly from a heart attack. I was in college and after receiving the news, travelled home to attend the funeral. One morning my sisters and I went to a local coffee shop where my Dad frequently visited. The men in the coffee shop, who knew of my Dad's death tried to comfort us and began to tell us stories about my Dad. The men talked about how my Dad constantly told everyone at the coffee shop about *his girls*, and how proud of them he was. I remember feeling anger and disappointment (that later sent me into counseling), that my Dad told every-one else how proud he was of me, but he never told me.

After the funeral, I left my hometown and returned to college determined to excel in every area of my life. I guess I felt I had something to prove to my Dad, and to everyone else. I spent the next few years torturing myself and played the game of comparison every chance I got. I compared myself to everyone, and when I found others *lower* than me, I felt good about myself, but I would look the other direction to see individuals much "better' than me, which sent me into a self-loathing pattern. What I was trying to prove was that I was good enough.

A few years later, when I eventually spiraled into clin-ical depression, counseling helped me deal with my in-securities. The process of counseling helped me work through some of the roots of my insecurities, and my need to compare. It has taken me years to become secure with whom I am in Christ, and honestly I still very much deal with this issue on a frequent basis.

Perhaps, you too have wounds that cause you to feel inadequate or insecure. Maybe these past hurts either stem from a parent, or from abuse. If you struggle with this issue and cannot seem to get a handle on it, I highly encourage you to seek out counseling so that you can work through these hurts. If counseling is not an option, find a trusted friend you can confide in.

Comparing yourself to others is a bottomless pit that will never bring you satisfaction or peace. Instead, look to the One who made you and designed you. Stand on what He says about you. We will never go wrong if we choose to believe what Christ says about us and keep our eyes focused on Him.

Self-Esteem

The Dangerous Game of Comparing

In my practice, I work with women who struggle with self-esteem. I believe that the battle most women have with their self image is one the enemy has a hay day with. The battle with self-esteem is rampant in our culture. You cannot pick up a magazine without seeing an article on *"how to improve your self-esteem."* Self help books have been written by the dozens in an attempt to answer the need to *"have better self esteem."*

As daughters of the Most High, why in the world do we struggle with our self esteem? It is the question of the century and yet the truth is we just do.

I run a group for teenage girls around the issue of self-image. These girls are beautiful, talented, smart, funny, but every week they sit around and discuss how much they don't like themselves. In eight weeks, which is the duration of the group, the goal is to help the girls learn to "be okay" with who they are and realize they do not have to compare and be like other girls. It seems simple enough and yet at the end of the eight weeks, though many see improvement in their self image, they are not magically cured. My point is, attaining a healthy self esteem takes time and due diligence to achieve.

At the risk of sounding like a self help book, I would like to offer three tips on how you can have a healthier view of **YOU**.

Focus On What You Can Do

Many of us spin our wheels focusing on all the things we can't do, and that gets us nowhere. We look at women in our lives that seem to have it all together and from the outside, don't appear to battle at all with self-esteem. The truth is, the women you compare yourself to probably also have the same struggles, which means they are most likely not the self assured confident women they portray themselves to be.

The game of comparing shows us all of the things we can't do and all of the ways we just do not measure up. Instead, stop looking at what you *can't* do and focus on what you *can* do.

Our worship director's wife Linda is quiet and reserved, and her husband Tony is the social, outgoing one. She is not loud and gregarious but she has such a heart for other people, and it shows. Linda has shared with me about how other people expect her to sing because her husband is the worship leader, but Linda does not sing. However, Linda is comfortable with this. Instead of focusing on what she *can't* do, she focuses on what she *can* do. Linda is an amazing hostess and cook and if you go to her house, you will feel welcomed by a hug and a smile as she ushers you into her home. In short, Linda is amazing and focuses on all the things she can do, instead of the one thing she can't do.

Learn to be comfortable with who you are, not who you think or other people think you should be. When you put your focus on what you can do, you will find freedom and fulfillment in the person God made you to be. Live in your sweet spot!

Who Do You Think You Are?

The mind is powerful and the thoughts that we allow ourselves to dwell on have the potential to either provide life or death. 2 Corinthians 10:5 says, "*We demolish arguments and every pretension that sets itself up against the knowledge of God; and we take captive every thought to make it obedient to Christ*" (NIV).

God knows of the struggle most of us have with our thought patterns and in this verse encourages us to not only watch our thoughts, but to be vigilant.

Several years ago, I worked with a woman in my practice as a therapist who had very low self-esteem. During one of our sessions, I made tally marks every time she called herself stupid. After 30 minutes, I stopped and shared how many tally marks I had made. The total was over 50! This woman was not shocked by the number because she basically viewed herself as stupid. I asked her how many times a day she estimated she called herself stupid or worthless. She replied, *"I probably can't count that high."*

I challenge you to become aware of your thoughts. How often do you put yourself down, or think of yourself as stupid, inadequate or worthless? Raise the antenna and become aware of negative thought patterns in your life and put a stop to them. Negative thoughts patterns will destroy you.

On the other hand, positive thoughts and meditating on what the Bible says about who you are will in turn revolutionize not only your thought life, but also your self-image. We are what we think.

Get Over the Need to Be Perfect

I'm just going to come out and say it. You are not perfect and you don't have to be! When we try to have the appearance of being perfect, it causes us to be fake and not genuine. Most of us have flirted with trying to be someone we are not and quite often; this ends in disaster leaving us feeling empty and hollow. Instead be real and be you.

In her book, "Fight Like a Girl," Lisa Bevere states, *"I think for a long time Christian women felt unreasonably pressured to appear perfect. This caused a lot of us to be unapproachable and not genuine. We foolishly imagined pretending to be perfect would inspire perfection, but rather than lifting others up, we weighed them down."* [2] This pressure to be perfect is probably one you can relate to as in ministry and church planting, the glass house syndrome impacts all of us, but people do not want perfection, they want authenticity.

You do not have to have it all together, all the time, my friend. It is perfectly acceptable to make mistakes and have imperfections. Many times, showing even a hint of these imperfections opens the door of freedom not only for you, but also for the people you minister to. When people see that their pastor's wife is not perfect but instead is a real woman, they feel free to be themselves as well.

Find freedom from the desire and need to be perfect. The sooner you do, the quicker you will find liberty to be real and will get out from under a fake shell. God has gifted you in unique ways that will impact many people, so get real and let Him accomplish much in you! Even Bruno Mars gets it in his song "Just The Way You Are," when he says, *"Girl, you're amazing, just the way you are."*

No Comparison

One of the things I love about church planting is that there is no previous pastor's wife for people to compare me to. One of our founding members fondly refers to me

---

[2] Bevere, Lisa, *Fight Like a Girl* : (New York, NY:Warner Faith, 2006). Pg. 164.

as the *"first lady,"* which makes me smile. As church planter's wives we are the *"first"* in our churches and there is freedom in this.

Some of my friends who are pastor's wives of existing churches talk about the comparison people in their churches make to previous pastor's wives. My heart goes out to these women as they seek to navigate the dangerous game of comparing and find freedom to be themselves. As a planter wife, this freedom naturally comes with planting a church.

When we decided to step out as lead pastors and plant a church, I determined I would be myself. I have maintained my realness and authenticity as just being Angie Hamp. One of the most flattering compliments I have received so far is, *"you are not like any pastor's wife I have ever known!"* When someone tells me this I laugh because it is so true. Even the people who have said this in a condescending or negative way don't get me down. Thankfully, there have been enough people who have balanced out those "haters," and have remarked about how refreshing it is that I am so real and that because of my authenticity, they feel free to be real too.

As a planter wife you get the privilege to set the course and teach people in your church about expectations he or she may develop about you. I have no qualms about asking people not to call us during dinner. In addition, I have no issue with telling people not to bother us on our day off, unless it is a true emergency. I have even had tough conversations with people who expected me to be their all-in-all, and gently informed them that although I love our church, it is my husband's job, I do not get paid for it, and cannot be at every function. Because there is no previous pastor's wife to compare me to, people are typically okay with me and my way of doing things. So embrace this season where you are not compared with a predecessor and be you!

Nothing Compares to You

The game of comparing is dangerous and leads to heartache and disappointment. My prayer and challenge to all of us as planter wives is that we not engage in the game of comparison but instead can find peace with who we are, and the ministries God has called us to.

In the end, it is not about the number people who attended your launch, or how rapidly your church grows. What does matter is whether or not you chose to keep your eyes focused on God and His plan for your life. God is more concerned with our willingness to follow Him, and our obedience to follow the path He set forth for us.

Be vigilant and when the game of comparison knocks on your door and asks you to *come out and play,* resist and instead turn your eyes and your heart toward Jesus. In His eyes, nothing compares to you.

Part II

Finding Balance: Marriage, Family, Ministry, Work

> Don't marry the person
> you think you can live
> with; marry only the
> individual you think you
> can't live without.
> ~Dr. James Dobson~

CHAPTER 5

The Other Woman--The Church

"That will never happen to us!" Jon and I adamantly agreed that our marriage would never become one of the scary statistics we read about as we began the journey of church planting. In *Pastors at Greater Risk*, H. B. London, Jr. writes about some alarming statistics among pastors, and says *"pastors have the second highest divorce rate among all professions."*[3] This statistic certainly demonstrates that ministry in general can place tremendous stress on a marriage, but how much more strain does planting a church put on the relationship of the

---

[3] London, H. B., Wiseman, Neil, Pastors at Greater Risk, (Ventura, CA: Regal Books From Gospel Light, 2003). Pg. 86.

planter and his spouse? I believe that planting a church has the potential to put even more stress and strain on the marriage of the planter.

More Than You Bargained For

The first few years of a new church will require more time, money, sweat, blood, and tears than you planned for. As we prepared for the launch of Discovery Church, Jon asked a wealthy business owner we knew for his best advice. He said, *"if you want to be successful, be prepared to spend endless hours working and very little time at home with your wife and family."* I frowned at this advice and yet as the lead planters, we are required to make sure all t's are crossed, and all the i's are dotted. This takes time—and a lot of it.

Starting a new church requires that every little detail, right down to providing diapers and wipes for the nursery is completed before launch. There is no ready-made package complete with everything you need for launch day. Preparation for a new church takes time, and not just a few hours a day. A church planter can literally spend weeks researching and making decisions on what type of sound system will best suit the church's needs. The point I am making is that all of these necessary preparations consume large blocks of time, making it very difficult to focus on the marriage relationship.

The Big One

Before our official grand opening, we had five monthly preview services leading to the big launch day. The first preview service was scheduled to be held on Easter Sunday, and we were very nervous about what that day would bring. In my efforts to be a good and supportive wife, I took note of the signs of weariness my husband showed as he worked long hours for months with no day off. I then formulated a plan to whisk our family away for a few days in the mountains following the first preview service. I envisioned the look of gratitude and surprise on my husband's face as I shared with him how I had planned two romantic days away on the ski slopes of beautiful Colorado. What husband wouldn't love that?

My bubble burst very quickly when my husband showed horror and fear at the revelation of my big surprise, rather than gratitude. I distinctly remember the sting I felt as he explained that leaving town after a preview was impossible because of all of the follow-up that needed to be done. I burst into tears of anger and hurt because, from my viewpoint, I had been extremely patient with him for months as he spent countless nights working on the church. My poor husband looked at me and reluctantly agreed to go on the surprise trip I had planned, but I could tell he felt torn.

Our time away turned out to be more stressful than rejuvenating as Jon spent the majority of the time either on the phone or returning e-mails, and I spent the time allowing resentment and anger to brew. On the last night of the trip I went to bed early, whereas Jon stayed out in the kitchen until late batting cleanup from the preview service. As I lay in bed, I reflected about how far off the path we were in terms of our marriage.

Before planting Discovery Church, our marriage was rock solid; we had a good balance between time for our marriage, and time for ministry. Within just a few months though, all that balance went out the window as we found ourselves distant, and frustrated with one another. It seemed the only topic that didn't cause tension was the church, which is ironic because planting the church is what had put the strain on our relationship.

I thought back to the statistic we read months earlier and gained a new understanding of why so many ministry marriages end in divorce. I even began to wonder if my marriage could become one of those sad statistics, and that night served as a huge wake up call.

I cried out to God and asked Him to help us restore some semblance of sanity and balance to our lives. I asked Him to help me be patient and loving, and to provide ways we could carve out time for our marriage. I so desperately missed my best friend, my partner, my lover, and I desired for our marriage to be restored to the amazing relationship we had before we planted a church.

As I prayed for wisdom and guidance, the Lord began to show me that my husband was not the enemy but that instead, he needed my partnership. As I allowed this perspective to sink in, and I prayed for more insight into what this concept meant, my heart softened toward Jon and I began to realize the pressure he was under.

Planting a church takes guts! All eyes were on us from different sides, many of which included those people who had invested financially into Discovery Church. Somewhere in the mix, I had allowed resentment, anger, and loneliness to settle into my heart, and had come to believe that Jon preferred the success of the church over the success of our marriage. This belief served to harden my heart until it all came to a head one night during a heated argument between Jon and me.

A Turning Point

I used to tease Jon and call his laptop *"the mistress."* One night we argued over the time he spent working versus time spent with me, and I called the church *"the other woman."* This term struck a chord in me and I later reflected on what caused those words to come out of my mouth. What I had to admit is that I honestly felt as though the church had replaced *me* in my husband's life. This concept may seem extreme and yet it encapsulated exactly how I felt. I shared my feelings with Jon, which he did not appreciate much at first, but the more he thought about what I shared, the more he understood how and why I thought that the church was *the other woman* in our lives.

That day marked the beginning of a turning point in our relationship. Although things did not change overnight, we rededicated ourselves to the commitment we made to put our marriage first, and slowly our relationship began to bloom again. God worked on my heart and Jon's during the next several months as we both worked to bring more balance into our marriage. During times Jon worked too many hours, I prayed for God to be near to him, and to help him handle the pressure. God also created opportunities for me to gently remind Jon that he was out of balance and that our marriage was suffering.

Another realization for us was that we both wanted the same things. We both desired a happy, healthy marriage and we both desired to plant a church. How these two purposes were accomplished often clashed, which caused conflict in our marriage. So we determined to find ways to be proactive to put the *other woman* in her place.

Maximize the Moments

I often complained to Jon that once we began the process of planting our church, we didn't date anymore. Not only was it difficult to find time, but finances were also an issue. One day, as I lamented about this to Jon, he offered something very profound. He said, *"Hon, we have to maximize the moments."* I have to admit I was quite annoyed with his *"wisdom,"* but as he provided suggestions on how to accomplish maximizing our moments, I became excited about the possibilities. Here are some ways we "maximize the moments" in our marriage.

Coffee Time

Jon and I purchased a nice coffee maker and started waking up a little earlier each morning. Each day, we take turns bringing coffee to bed and enjoy drinking it together before the busyness of the day sets in. This continues to be one of my favorite times with my husband.

Text Sweet Nothings

This day and age provides technology as a means to maximizing moments. There have been many times when the Lord moves on me to send my husband an encouraging text, and in return, the Lord often moves on Jon to do the same. Just this simple form of communication is an excellent pathway to maximize a few moments a day with your spouse.

Romantic Walks

This seems simple enough and yet many of us do not take advantage of the beauty of the outdoors. Walking hand-in-hand with your spouse can set the stage for conversation and romance! Our romantic walks have generated many discussions about our future hopes and dreams as well as time for us to get some exercise and take a breather from life.

Lunch Dates

We set aside one day a week to have lunch together. Thankfully, the lunch menu at restaurants is much cheaper than the dinner menu. Taking time out of the workweek to share a meal, preferably with no children, is a great way to maximize some moments with your husband. I encourage you to check your local papers or websites for coupons so that you can try new restaurants. Be adventurous!

Plan a Vacation

You may laugh at the prospect of this suggestion but don't turn a deaf ear just yet. There are ways to go on vacation, even when you are planting a church.

The year we planted our church also happened to be the year of our 15-year wedding anniversary, and Jon and I desperately desired to go on a cruise. So we started stashing away money; 10 dollars here, 20 there until we had enough to buy our cruise. We also sold items around our house on Craigslist to pay for the trip. We asked my in-laws to watch our children for an entire week so we could really maximize some moments together, and enjoyed an entire week aboard a cruise ship making precious memories together. Currently, we are in the process of stashing away money for our next vacation together.

If taking a cruise is not an option for you, there are numerous accommodations provided to ministers for little or no cost. Parsonage.org, which is a website of Focus on the Family, provides a list of free and low-cost retreats for ministers. I encourage you to look into some options, so that you can maximize many moments with your spouse. If you are battling guilt at the prospect of taking a vacation because you are a church planter, I encourage you to put these thoughts from the enemy out of your mind. Investing in your marriage is crucial.

I challenge you to find ways to maximize the moments in your marriage. Going on expensive dates or carving out large portions of time is not always feasible however, there are those moments in life, which are precious and can serve to both rejuvenate and fill your tank. Precious moments spent together also serve to provide balance between you and the *other woman*" and also open lines of communication that clog due to resentment and lack of quality time spent together.

Communication

Typically, we as women enjoy talking more than men do, and are often the ones that have our antennae raised, so to speak, if communication is not flowing in the relationship.

In my work as a therapist, most couples who seek out marriage counseling report that the number one issue in their relationship is a lack of good communication. The concept of communication seems quite simple on the surface, but when emotions are running high, and resentment, loneliness, and anger are thrown in the mix, a cocktail for poor communication exists. Add to that, memories of arguments that spring up out of failed attempts at communication and the process of effective communication is further complicated.

In the months preceding the launch of Discovery Church, Jon and I conflicted very frequently and to be brutally honest, all the communication skills I teach my clients were thrown out the window in my own marriage. I found myself being the kind of wife I vowed to never be, and this caused my husband to tune me out. He spent the majority of his days listening to other people and solving all the issues in the church, and then often came home to an unhappy wife, who needed to vent about the day and its problems. Let me clarify that sharing problems and concerns with your husband is not wrong and because it is a partnership, a team approach should definitely be in place in a marriage relationship. Where the issue lies is in *how* we communicate the information.

Remember earlier when I shared that during an argument the words *"other woman"* toppled out of my mouth? The accusation and comparison of the church being the *other woman* came from the pangs of loneliness and deep hurt I had about feeling replaced by the church plant. Initially the declaration of feelings I made were laced with icy, bitter words, and immediately put Jon on the defensive. This strategy was certainly not a form of effective communication, but as I mentioned earlier, this "fight" served as a turning point in our relationship. The reason is because I got to the heart of exactly what was going on with me and consequently, after some time of prayer and reflection, I communicated my feelings without hurling accusations at my husband. My approach the second time around was much different and to my delight, Jon responded with compassion, took responsibility for his part and agreed to work on changes. It was miraculous!

I realize that good communication sounds easy and yet it is not an easy skill to master. Effective communication in a marriage takes work on the parts of *both* people. The problem is that in the middle of a heated argument, the ability to think and reason rationally is very difficult, which is why it is crucial to take some time to process what is going on inside of you.

Below are three layers of communication, with a three-step approach for each. With practice and patience your marriage can experience renewed and effective communication.

Layer One of Communication – Discovery

The **first layer** of effective communication involves discovering exactly *what* you feel and *why* you feel it before relaying the information to your spouse. Here is a simple three-step approach.

1. **What Are You Feeling?** Write down all the emotions you feel about a particular situation.
2. **Why Do You Feel This Way?** Write down the reasons.
3. **Pray For Wisdom and Direction** –When you know what and why you feel a certain way, ask God for help in dealing with the hurts and the situation.

How many times have you regretted the words that "slipped" out during an argument? Following this approach will help to eliminate some of those words we wish we could eat. Sometimes we direct feelings of anger and frustration at our spouses that are issues we need to work on. That is why the final step of prayer is so crucial. When we to go to God with the what's and why's He never fails to provide insight into the situation.

James 1:5 sums it up best and says, *If any of you lacks wisdom, he should ask God, who gives generously to all without finding fault, and it will be given to him* (NIV). He is also faithful to give you the right words to speak when the time comes to speak your husband during the second layer of communication. Again, this layer consists of a simple three-step approach.

Layer Two of Communication
Productive Talk

1. **Use "I" statement** rather than **"you" statements**. Own how you feel.
2. **Watch Your Tone of Voice**
3. **Use The Sandwich Approach** – start with a positive, "sandwich" in your concerns, end with a positive.

As you read this it may occur to you that this sounds very exhausting! Effective communication takes work but is worth it and will improve your marriage in amazing ways. Though cumbersome at first, with practice, these steps will become second nature and require less effort to execute.

Layer Three of Communication
Follow-Through and Accountability

The strategies and tips presented are good in theory and may work for a time but what happens when both you and your spouse begin to slip back into old patterns of communication? With this, the third layer of communication becomes crucial. I call this layer, **follow-through and accountability.**

Most of us have every intention of staying on the straight and narrow initially but often, life happens and we discard the commitments we made to change our ways.

This happened to Jon and me on many occasions, so it was necessary to implement the third layer of communication where we gave each other permission to be accountable when either of us "slipped" with the follow through portion.

A word of caution about the third layer of communication: It is important that trust is developed so that when accountability is provided it is received in the right way. For example, if you tend to use "you" statements with a bitter tone of voice during layer two, it is unlikely that when you provide accountability, your spouse will be receptive. Again, the approach is crucial when implementing this step.

1. **Avoid Sarcasm** – Refrain from statements like, "I knew you wouldn't follow through." Or you must not care about our marriage."
2. **Gentle Reminders** – This tactic should serve to "remind" both of you to remain true to changes you agree to make. Try saying things like, "I miss you honey. Can we schedule a lunch date?" or "It seems we're both falling back into our old patterns. What are some ways we can get back on track?"

3. **Provide Affirmation** – When your spouse does follow through or makes a point to turn off their phone or computer, make sure you affirm them. Reinforcement is certain to encourage even more follow through!

Additional Tips

AVOID discussing anything of great importance after 9:00 p.m.

H.A.L.T. If you are **hungry, angry, lonely** or **tired,** take care of these needs before discussing difficult issues.

AVOID the Doorknob Syndrome – Do not start a conversation as your husband is walking out the door, instead carve out time where you can focus on the situation at hand.

Effective Communication

Effective communication takes work and practice. Do not be discouraged if you do not always get it right; however, strive to be diligent in achieving this very important skill to keep the "other woman" in her place.

On the following page is a simple chart of the layers of communication to help keep communication on track in your marriage.

Layer One	• **Discovery** • What Do I Feel? Prayer for wisdom
Layer Two	• **Productive Talk** • I statements, Watch tone, Sandwich
Layer Three	• **Follow Through/Accountability** • No sarcasm, Reminders/Affirmation

A Fulfilling Marriage

Today you may be dealing with resentment and anger. Perhaps your marriage is experiencing stress and distance as you navigate the first few years of planting a church, and the changes that are inevitable in the journey. Maybe you are lonely and frustrated that the church seems to be *the other woman* in your relationship.

John 10:10 says, *"The thief comes to steal, kill and destroy"* (NIV). Your marriage is one of Satan's targets so be vigilant and fight! The second half of this verse declares that *"I have come that you might have life and have it to the full."* (NIV).

This fullness Christ spoke of can happen once again in your marriage. My friend, no matter where you are at, no matter how much hurt or anger you may have, Jesus stands ready to assist you. He desires to bind up the wounds, bring life to your marriage, and help you keep *the other woman* in her rightful place.

> I am woman! I am
> invincible! I am pooped!
> ~Author Unknown~

CHAPTER 6

Jumping Back into the Workplace
Balancing family, church and work

Most of us don't go into ministry believing we will ever obtain great wealth, but the need to pay the bills is a reality. Typically, the salary of a planter is not enough to provide adequately for the family, so many planter wives work outside of the home to help provide for the family's finances.

During the writing of this book, I conducted a poll of 13 church planters' wives and asked them if church planting required that they work outside of the home to help provide for the family. Out of the 13 women polled, 11 reported that they had to work so that their husbands could plant a church. All of the women reported that the salary their husbands received from the church was not nearly enough to provide for the family. The women polled also reported that in addition to working outside of the home, they also administrated ministries in the church.

Securing a job can be difficult and adds just one more task to the already full plate of a planter wife. This can create an endless juggling act of balancing marriage, family, ministry, and work. However, most planter wives are so dedicated and committed to the call of church planting that they take on all of these tasks with strength and dignity.

Planter wives manage households, run ministries in the church and are diligent workers at their jobs. Because church planter wives are willing to work outside of the home, their husbands can focus on the church, which in turn provides a much higher survivability rate.

Often planter wives find themselves strung out, weary, and pulled in every different direction as they sacrifice their own emotional, mental, and spiritual health. There is hope however, and ways you can balance the juggling act of family, ministry and work without losing your sanity.

Back to Work

At the beginning of this chapter, I cited an informal poll, where 11 of the 13 church planter wives worked outside of the home because their husbands were church planters. Many of the women in this study were stay-at-home Moms prior to church planting, but had to seek out employment when their husbands planted a church.

The women in the poll reported two main challenges in their search for a job. First, they needed jobs that provided flexible hours so they could juggle family and ministry. Second, the job needed to provide adequate pay so the planter wife could contribute significantly to the family finances.

Perhaps you are up against the same challenges. The reality may loom large for you and your husband, that planting a church will require you to work outside of the home. This reality can be discouraging and daunting as you foresee the difficulties working outside of the home can present.

If church planting requires you to find additional sources of income, and you are overwhelmed at the prospect of balancing family, ministry and work; there is hope, and God stands ready to provide you with that perfect job.

The Perfect Job

The study conducted among 13 church planter wives asked the question of what types of jobs the women worked. Some women worked at Starbucks, others were teachers, some worked at daycares so their children could go to work with them, and some found work-from-home positions. Some church planter wives worked part-time whereas others worked full-time. So how does one land that perfect job?

Pray

The first step in looking for a job is to pray. This could go without saying, but in your role as a church planter's wife you need a job that will serve many needs. You need to make a certain amount of money, have flexibility and would preferably like to enjoy your work. This type of job description is difficult to find and yet when we seek God and ask him to open the right door, He will.

One church planter's wife shared that she desperately needed a job that would allow her to be at home with her children, so she began to pray and seek God. Out of the blue, God sent her a nanny job that allowed her to make money, and stay at home with her children.

Another church planter's wife reported that God opened the door for her to teach again. The job allowed her to be on the same schedule as her children, provided good benefits and gave her weekends, holidays, and summers off with her family.

God sees your willingness to work so that your husband can plant a church, and He will provide the right job for you.

Ask Family and Friends

A second way to land that perfect job is to talk to family and friends. Sometimes, getting a referral from someone who is an "insider" can open doors of opportunity you would not normally have, just from looking for work in the classifieds, or on Craigslist. Ask members of your launch team or neighbors if they know of anyone hiring. You would be surprised at how many people don't put out ads, but instead prefer direct referrals.

What Do You Like To Do?

A third tip for landing that perfect job is to think about what you enjoying doing. Maybe you believe you have few skills, or do not have a degree that would enable to you to secure a good job. Instead of thinking about what you cannot do, think about what you can do. Use the skills and talents God gave you and look for a job that utilizes hose abilities.

Maybe you are good at arranging flowers. If so, look for a job in a floral shop. Perhaps you are good with children. Seek out employment at a Mom's Day Out program or watch children in your home. If you are organized and have a knack for office work, look for a job as an administrative assistant.

The point is you are a talented, capable woman, so use the abilities you already have, as you seek out employment. God cares about your situation and knows your need of the perfect job.

Worn-out, Weary and Pulled In Every Different Direction

There is no doubt that along this road of church planting you have experienced times you felt weary and pulled in a hundred different directions. Church planter wives inevitably struggle with balance as they juggle all the roles that come with the territory of church planting. Most days in the life of a planter wife start very early and end late. The days are long, and the list to be done is even longer, which can leave you exhausted. It is crucial to take care of you, and yet self care very often gets put on the back burner as wives attempt to take care of everything and everyone else. When this happens for too long, burnout is inevitable.

The potential for burnout in church planting is exceptionally high. Even though we like to think ourselves as superhuman, the truth is we are human and can only handle high loads of stress for so long before we either spiral downward into depression or fizzle out.

In his book, "Pastors at Greater Risk," H.B. London cites the statistic that *"45% of pastor's wives say the greatest danger to them and family is physical, emotional, mental*

and spiritual burnout.".[4] When you feel physically, emotionally, mentally, and spiritually drained for an ex-
tended periods, you are at a high risk for burnout. The
truth is planting a church requires wives to handle high
loads of stress; it unfortunately just comes with the territory.

In my journey as a planter wife, I can speak firsthand
to high levels of stress. I had to return to work after being a stay-at-home Mom for years so that we could plant
a church. I currently work two jobs, including running
my own business, coordinate ministries at our church,
run our household, and am raising two young boys. In
addition, I still have the responsibility of volunteering at
my kids' schools, and maintaining friendships. Sometimes it is just too much! I often want to go sit in a corner
in my room, rock back and forth, and cry about the stress
load I carry. Some weeks I work every day, and then
spend my weekends involved in church activities, only
to begin the whole cycle again on Monday. As you read
this, you are probably shaking your head because your
week is somewhat identical to mine.

Can't You Do Something Else?

There have been times when I wished my husband
did something else for a living. According to surveys
conducted by the Global Pastors Wives Network
(GPWN), *eight out of ten pastor's wives wish their husbands
would choose a different profession.[5]* Perhaps you have had

---

[4] London, H. B., Wiseman, Neil, Pastors at Greater Risk, (Ventura, CA: Regal Books
From Gospel Light, 2003). Pg. 118.

[5] Pastors Wives Come Together: Cullen Takeuchi, Li-
sa:http://time.com/time/magazine/article/0,9171,1604902-1,00.html

this thought as well. At the core, most pastors' wives want their husbands to answer God's call. Church planter wives are no exception, and work harder than any other group of people I have ever met, but sometimes the load we carry, the amount of stress, and the duration of such a season is just too much.

Many Sunday mornings I have driven to church and watched neighbors playing in the yard, or people at the park and longed to be a normal person who skipped Sundays to do what I wanted to do. There are times when I have looked at my husband and his talents and wondered how much money he could make in a secular job. Because of my schedule, I have missed some of my children's events, lunch with my friends and overall quality of life. Some days I feel so completely depleted and bone tired that I can't fathom getting through another day.

Perhaps you feel the same way and wonder how you will keep up with the pace that your current reality demands. Maybe working a job outside of the home has put you over the top, and you are already either in burnout mode, or are well on your way.

It is normal to feel worn-out, weary, and pulled in every different direction, but there are ways to effectively manage your stress load and balance work, family, and ministry.

Prioritization and Boundaries
Two Keys For Sanity

Before you begin reading this section, grab a notebook and a pen. At the top of the page, write *Priorities* on one side and *Boundaries* on the other side. Draw a line down the middle of the page. Then make a list of the top five;

yes I said five priorities in your life. You will be tempted to write down 15 or 20 priorities, but I want to challenge you to keep it to just five.

Next, define your five priorities a bit more. For example, if you listed quality family time as one of your priorities, create a subcategory for what quality family time means. This might include the creation of a family night once per week where you play a game, or watch a movie.

On the other side of the page, make a list of five boundaries that you need to put into place to keep your priorities. Boundaries are critical if you want to keep your priorities.

Here is an example of my priority and boundary list. It has helped me tremendously in the balancing act.

Priorities	**Boundaries**
Time With God	Shut Out Distractions
Quality Family Time	No phone, email, facebook
Self Care	No martyr syndrome or guilt
Writing/ Ministry to Women	Jon cooks dinner once a week/ cares for kids
Quality Work	Max. 40 hours or work

Setting priorities and drawing boundaries are two major keys to balancing work, family, and ministry. It is impossible to do everything and be everything to everybody all the time. If you've ever been burned out, you probably vowed to never return to that place again, yet the slope to burnout is slippery and fast if we do not prioritize and set boundaries. Prioritization and boundaries are not your foe, they are your friends and will keep you sane, healthy, and balanced.

All in a Day's Work

Although holding down a job outside of the home is taxing and tiring, it also can be satisfying and can boost confidence and self image. Many planters wives report a high level of satisfaction in knowing that because they work outside the home and help provide for the family, their husbands can focus full-time on the church plant.

One planter wife told me that she enjoys her job and is able share her faith and rub shoulders with unbelievers. She also reported that working has given her the opportunity to use skills and talents that lay dormant for years, and that getting compliments and affirmation from co-workers and supervisors has served to boost her confidence. Other planter wives also report that working outside of the home has made them more disciplined with their time as well, and that they use ideas implemented at work in the church also.

Another planter wife shared with me that God used her job as a way to help provide a donation to their church. The company she worked for gave a matching donation to a few nonprofit organizations and because this wife had been a diligent worker, she felt confident in asking that the church be the recipient of the donation.

Other planter wives reported they were able to lead coworkers to Christ, and invited numerous people to church. In a way, the workforce can be our own personal mission field if we allow God to use us in that way. In ministry, we often fellowship with believers and yet working in a secular environment opens doors of ministry we would not have otherwise, to share Christ with those who do not know Him.

Keeping Your Eyes on the Prize

Sometimes the best way to get through a difficult season in life is to keep a healthy perspective. Our lives have seasons and seasons change. Right now, you are probably in one of the busiest seasons of your life as you attempt to balance family, ministry, and work. Perhaps you feel overwhelmed at what is expected of you and the amount of stress you carry daily. Maybe, burnout looms large, and threatens you on a frequent basis.

As you navigate this season of your life, keep your eyes focused on the prize. Remember that what you do daily should not be just for others, but should be worship to God. He is our prize.

Your sacrifice and willingness to work outside the home so that your husband can plant a church is commendable and recognized by God. You may feel unappreciated and frustrated at times, especially at the end of a 16-hour day, but as you seek to please God instead of just the people around you, your perspective--the right perspective will take shape. God is pleased with you, friend.

Take time to care for yourself and set priorities and boundaries so that you can balance all of the daily tasks on your to-do list. This season of your life, though busy may be one you look back on with fond memories. Let God use you in your job to accomplish great things for Him. Ask Him to give you the right perspective and to open doors of opportunity for that perfect job.

Deuteronomy 15:10 says, *"Give generously to him and do so without a grudging heart; then because of this the LORD your God will bless you in all your work and in everything you put your hand to"* (NIV). Our God is faithful and will reward your diligence and obedience as you seek to honor Him.

> Raising a kid is part joy
> and part guerilla warfare.
> ~Ed Asner~

CHAPTER 7

What About My Kids?

Church Planting Can Be Positive and Fun For Your Kids!

Children are a gift from God. Ask any Mom how she feels about her children, and she will quickly list several ways her children are amazing, special and gifts from above. As you read this, you are probably thinking about how much you love your children and how special they are to you.

You probably also have concerns about how church planting will impact, or has already impacted your little treasures. God has placed in all of us a "momma bear" type of instinct that longs to protect our young. As women, we are intuitive, and can sense when our children are happy, or when they are sad. We take great care to make sure our children are fed, clothed, clean, content, and happy, however church planting can threaten many of the needs that our children have.

The reality is that church planting changes everything. Many times, children have to leave the church they grew up in, move to a different house, in a different town, attend a new school, and make new friends. These are all major life changes kids have to adjust to. In addition, kids sense the stress and tension their parents are under and often have to sacrifice time with their Moms and Dads so that church planting can be accomplished. Sadly, there are times our children get put on the back burner.

As a planter wife, God called you to minister to others, but first and foremost He called you to minister to your children. Church planting constantly demands our attention, focus, and time. Church planting can be a positive and exciting venture for you and your kids, and can open doors for incredible memories to be made. We do have to be careful though because unfortunately many pastor's kids grow up resenting church and God.

Why Pastors Kids Hate Church

Pastor's kids are often the butt of jokes and have a reputation for being rebellious and unruly. Unfortunately, many pastor's kids often hate the ministry and can't wait to leave church once they are adults. In our years of ministry we have talked with many pastor's kids who wished their parents weren't in ministry and don't even like church. Many pastors' kids struggle with resentment, and anger because of the unrealistic expectations placed on them by their parents, and people in the church. Pastor's kids feel an enormous amount of pressure to be perfect, spiritual all the time, and be a good example to others.

In her book, "Being a Minister's Wife and Being Your

self," Nancy Parnell candidly writes about kids and ministry. She says, *"Apparently, God did not know minister's children were supposed be perfect. He did not give us perfect children."*[6] I am sure your children and mine are about as close to perfect as perfect gets. In ministry, people (parents included) have unrealistic expectations for pastors' kids.

I believe that God is calling us to turn the tide and help to change the perceptions and viewpoints people have of pastors' kids. Church planting provides this opportunity to shift the tide, because it allows us to set the precedent in our churches about expectations for our kids. Once kids feel free to be themselves and just be regular kids, the trend of hating church and ministry will change.

As planter wives, we have the challenge and honor of raising our kids in the church. I propose that the years spent as pastors' kids can be a time when we make good memories, as we seek to allow our kids to thrive and be who God called them to be, instead of what other people expect them to be.

Draw a Line in the Sand

One way to turn the tide of unrealistic expectations is to watch our own expectations of our kids. Sometimes, I think we unconsciously expect our kids to behave and be perfect little robots, especially at church.

God has used my kids on many occasions to teach me lessons. During the pre-launch phase of our church, we traveled around to different churches to raise money for

---

[6] Parnell, Nancy, *Being a Minister's Wife and Being Yourself*, (Nashville, TN: Broadman Press, 1993). Pg 28.

the church plant. My poor kids had to endure many long services, and although we tried to make it fun, they would have preferred to stay home. Before we went into a church, we would turn around in the car and give our kids "**the lecture**."

It went something like this: *"Now you guys better behave and we mean it. We are here raising money for the church so be polite to people, and make good eye contact. If you are good, we will get you a treat later, okay?"* The boys would give us a glazed look as they hesitantly shuffled into the church and did their robotic, my Mom and Dad are church planters duty.

One Sunday, we attended a smaller church that had worship that was less than pleasing to the ears. My boys fidgeted in their seats as the worship service neared 45 minutes. The worship was grueling to all of us, much less two young boys, and I knew that eventually something was going to come out of one of their mouths.

Just as we thought the worship service was ending, the leader felt *"led of the Spirit"* to sing *"just one more song."* Suddenly, my youngest said quite loudly, "**NO! Not another song, please!**" Everyone heard and shot us dirty glances, although a few people chuckled. I started to turn around to scold my son, but as soon as I saw his face, I began to laugh uncontrollably. I couldn't stop laughing and eventually had to take my son out because *I* was being the disruptive one.

My poor little boy did not know what to do as I dragged him out of the church while trying to keep my laughter quiet. I am sure he thought he was going to get a spanking but instead, I pulled him onto my lap and we laughed together. We still laugh about that day, and recall the memory together.

Kids should be expected only to do so much. They are

kids and are not superhuman beings. If your child mis-behaves in church, discipline him or her the way other people would. If people tell you how you should raise your kids or begin to put ridiculous expectations on them, let the "momma bear" in you rise up and draw a line in the sand. Your kids will appreciate that you stood up for them and will remember how you let them just be normal kids. Your kids do not have to be perfect, so make sure your own expectations of them are realistic and when others seek to place expectations on your kids, set a boundary.

Get Your Kids Involved

A year into our church plant, I asked my kids how they felt about the church. They had a few criticisms, but overall both of my boys reported that they loved Discov-ery Church! I asked them what they loved about our church and they answered, "*it is awesome*" and we get to do really "*fun stuff*" at church. This made me smile be-cause my boys are involved with many ministries at the church. All along, it has been their choice what they want to be involved in.

From day one, Jon and I made planting the church a family venture, and it most certainly has been that. Church planting can be a dream the entire family can be a part of; even your kids.

Our boys were eight and ten when we began the process of church planting and from the beginning; we asked their opinions and involved them in as many deci-sions as we could.

Here are just a few ways you can involve your child-ren in church planting and make it a positive experience.

Help Them Discover Their Talents

Church planting opens the doors for you to help your kids discover their unique gifts and talents. Your children can use their gifts and talents in amazing ways in the church plant. One simple way to help them find their gifts is to simply ask them what they like to do.

My son Noah (age 12) has quite the knack for technology and computers. My husband Jon needed someone to run Pro Presenter for our pre launch services, but everyone one else on our launch team was involved in other areas. One night, we were discussing the need for a tech person and Noah, who knows a Mac computer from the inside out, asked if he could run Pro Presenter. He was only 10 at the time, and we were a little hesitant, but Jon said yes to him. Jon and Noah spent time together practicing as Jon played the worship songs for Noah and he ran the slides. To this day, Noah still runs Pro Presenter for our worship services, and he is good at it! He loves it and is an integral part of our Sunday morning team.

Our youngest son, Caleb (Age 10) has discovered his talent in helping others, and he assists our Children's director with the set-up and tear-down of the kids' classes. Caleb knows where everything goes and takes his job very seriously. Some of our set-up team refer to him as "the beast" because he carries heavy equipment in and out of the building each week. Caleb loves this nickname and also is an integral part of our team.

Help your kids discover their unique talents and gifts. Not only will this discovery help boost their self-esteem and confidence, but it will also incorporate them into church planting. In addition, it will make them feel a part of the team, rather than just giving them the sense that the church plant is "Mom and Dad's job."

Involve Your Kids in Decisions

The town where we planted our church has a median age of 34, which means that most people have children. Our goal was to meet a community need and provide an exciting and fun, ministry to children. One day we were discussing Kids' ministry in the car, when it occurred to me that perhaps we should ask our boys what they wanted to see in a Kids' Ministry at our church. They immediately came up with very creative ideas and as we began to view Kids' Ministry through the lenses of our children, a very cool, and fun plan formed.

When we looked at catalogs or went to furniture stores, we involved our kids and asked their opinions. They provided great feedback and many of the events or activities done in our kids department came from the ideas of our children.

I realize kids cannot be involved in all decisions, but they still can have feedback about many of the decisions made for the church. We all like to be asked our opinions and kids are no exception. When possible, ask your kids for their ideas and opinions. You just might be surprised at the creativity and well thought out ideas they have.

Don't Make Your Kids Go To Everything

Many planter wives feel the pressure to attend every function, activity, and event associated with church. Sometimes, we expect our children to attend all these events as well. This can leave your child feeling frustrated and resentful. Maybe you just need someone to tell you that your child does not have to go to every church event. Kids need to be kids and don't want to go to church activities every night of the week or on the weekends when they have time off from school.

Respect your children enough to allow them down time. If you and your husband have to attend an event, get a babysitter or make arrangements with friends so that your kids can just be kids. As their Mom, it is okay for you to stay home and miss events from time to time. You may feel the guilt or the push/pull syndrome but do what is best for your children. Remember, the church is not first in your life, your kids are. Take time to make them a priority.

I realize this is a difficult balance to strike, especially in the beginning stages of the church plant. The pre-launch phase of church planting is grueling. If you're not preparing for a pre-launch service, then you're out travelling and raising money.

One Saturday night, my kids were in a very grumpy mood as I explained the following morning's schedule for them. The plan was to get up at 5:30 a.m., leave the house by 6:00 a.m., attend two services, have lunch with the Pastor of the church, and drive two hours back home. My kids were not happy about this schedule and complained about how we *"make them go to everything."* After listening to them, I began to see their point of view. They went to school five days a week for seven to eight hours a day, and then had to spend their weekends doing church activities. My poor kids!

My husband, who also listened to the perspective of our kids, informed me that he would go to the church services by himself so I could stay home with the boys. The windows rattled as my kids shouted for joy and proclaimed their dad to be the *"best dad ever!"* I appreciated the opportunity to stay home and hang out with my boys. That Sunday was awesome as we declared it "pajama day" and spent precious time together relaxing and hanging out. I am sure people at the church my husband attended grumbled at bit at me not being there, but the reward of letting my boys just be at home and enjoy a day off was well worth it.

It is perfectly acceptable to let your kids' miss some church events and in fact, can be healthy and positive! Balance is the key and acquiring the right balance between church life, and a life for your kids will most certainly help keep church planting a positive experience for your children.

Real Advice from Church Planter's Kids

Recently, my oldest son Noah, who is 12, asked me if we were ever going to plant another church. I responded to him by asking why he wanted to know. He replied, *"Church planting is fun Mom, and I think it would be great to plant another church. "* I was dumbfounded and pleased at the same time that church planting had been a positive experience for him.

I probed a bit further into why he felt church planting had been so fun and he listed off several reasons.

Here are some of the things Noah liked, and disliked about planting a church--in his own words:

What I Like:
- Meeting new people
- You get good relationships out of it
- People go with the flow and have fun.

What I Don't Like:
- When people leave – it hurts my heart
- It is stressful

Advice to Church Planters – Noah Hamp, Age 12

"You should make sure your children don't feel left out and don't always give all of your attention to the church plant. Keep your morale high as best you can, because you're gonna make mistakes, and times will be tough, but life in church planting isn't fair."

Caleb wanted to give his feedback as well, and here are his thoughts:

Caleb Hamp, Age 10

What I Like:
- It's fun!
- I get to help my Dad a lot.
- I have the best kids church teacher.
- I love having people at our house a lot.

What I Don't Like:
- Sometimes had too many kids at our house.
- Sometimes I just wanted my mom and Dad to myself and I always had to share them.
- I did not like going to other churches that had bad music and long church services.

Advice to Church Planters – Caleb Hamp – Age 10

"Don't be afraid to ask people to go to your church. You should ask neighbors and friends everyday to go to church so they can find Jesus. Be very creative at your church and don't make it boring. No one wants to go to a boring church. If someone has a baby, you should make them great food. Be nice to everyone at church even when you feel like punching them."

Kids Rock at Church Planting

Our kids are the most valuable members of our team. They are honest, real, and are an asset to the church plant. Church planting can be an incredible journey for your kids and as you seek to provide balance, nurture their talents and gifts, you in turn get to see the blessing and reward of watching your kids be used of God. Who knows? You just might be raising up a new generation of church planters who will impact generations for Jesus.

> Your living is determined
> not so much by what life
> brings to you as by what
> you bring to life.
> ~Unknown~

CHAPTER 8

Riding the Roller Coaster without Tossing Your Cookies

Managing the ups and downs of church planting

One of my favorite places to vacation is California Adventure Park, which is attached to Disneyland. California Adventure Park hosts one of the fastest and most thrilling roller coasters, called "The California Screamin." The ride starts off at a complete stop and a sweet little voice counts down, 5..4..3..2..1 as the riders wait in anticipation of what comes next. Suddenly, the ride goes from zero to 55 miles in four seconds. Taking off that fast and that quickly makes the rider's stomach do a somersault, and true to its name the rider--**Screams**! The whole ride is set to music as the car dips up and down, and even loops upside down. At the end of the ride, a camera snaps a picture as hair flies wildly in the wind, and contorts the face in ways that simply are not flattering. The roller coaster is a rush!

My family and I love the California Screamin coaster, and in one trip rode the ride 11 times in a row. After riding the roller coaster that many times with the ups and downs, and twists and turns, I felt nauseated. The rest of the day, my entire equilibrium was off and I felt as if I was going to toss my cookies. My family and I took a break from the roller coaster, ate lunch and relaxed on less strenuous rides for the remainder of the day. After a couple of hours the nausea subsided, and I enjoyed the rest of our time at Disneyland.

Church planting is very much like a roller coaster. There are extreme highs and valleys so low, they are hard to rebound from. In addition, there are twists, turns, and seasons of trials, and difficulties. Most of us can handle periods of life that are hard for awhile, but after significant time passes, it becomes increasingly difficult to manage the highs, and lows without becoming discouraged to the point that we just *want off the ride*.

Church planting is inevitably a roller coaster and a ride you will never experience anywhere else, but there are ways to ride the roller coaster of church planting without *tossing your cookies*.

FACT: Church Planting Is an Emotional Roller Coaster

People often define women as emotional. Sometimes emotions are steady, and even-keeled but other times our emotions are all over the place. Church planting will inevitably trigger an emotional roller coaster like one you have never experienced before. In fact, in this journey your emotions may change from one moment to the next, leaving you with emotional whiplash!

On my journey of church planting I've encountered obstacles but have also seen God perform miracles. On one particular day, I rode the roller coaster of emotions so much that I felt like a rag doll by the end of the day. We had just officially launched our church and everything was going very well. My husband and I were sitting together, going through new connection cards and praising God for all the new people he had sent to our church. We were riding high, baby.

Then the phone rang. On the other line was the representative for the facility we were leasing calling to inform us that they did not desire to have us in their building any longer, and were choosing to break the lease. They also informed us that we had one week to find another facility.

In a matter of a few minutes, we went from riding high to a very scary low. We were six weeks into the life of our church and suddenly we were without a home. My husband and I spent the next hour in shock as we reeled from the devastating news. Knowing that we had to pick ourselves up and find a new church home, we sank to our knees in prayer. God gave my husband the idea to check into our local theater, and within just a few hours we toured the theater, and secured a new home for Discovery Church. Once again we were riding high as God performed an incredible miracle in a just a few short hours. Inevitably, though more lows followed.

The point is, church planting will be an emotional roller coaster. The key is to learn how to navigate the emotions of the roller coaster so that you do not lose heart and want to give up completely.

Riding the Highs and Lows

We've already established that church planting is an emotional roller coaster. We have also acknowledged that we as women are emotional beings who feel on a deep level. The question that remains though is how do we as women, who are emotional creatures ride the highs and lows associated with church planting in a way that honors God, and allows us to keep our mental health intact?

One way to navigate the emotional roller associated with church planting is simply to let yourself feel the emotions. Sometimes we minimize or play down feelings about situations, and become numb. The biggest reason for this is that allowing ourselves to feel the emotions associated with excitement or disappointment is uncomfortable and a bit scary, especially when you have ridden the highs and lows of church planting for awhile.

About four months after the launch of our church I began to feel flat and numb. When my husband told me something exciting that was happening in the church, I would try my best to muster up enthusiasm but just couldn't seem to show much. When he shared difficulties or obstacles, I just couldn't provide much compassion or concern regarding the situation. After a few weeks of the numb feeling, it dawned on me that I was just sick and tired of the roller coaster of emotions so I unconsciously determined that it was much easier to just not feel anything. My reasoning was that it was just too hard to recover from the extreme highs and lows, so I came to the conclusion it was much more logical to get off the roller coaster and instead, just be numb. It sounded like a great plan except that I felt hollow and empty. *Not* feeling went completely against the grain of who I was as a woman, and as Angie. You see, I feel deeply, I love deeply. I live life with passion and feeling the emotions associated with a life of passion, and the inevitable roller coaster is just part of the deal.

My encouragement is to ride the highs when they are there. When things in your church plant are going well, allow yourself to celebrate. Do not hold back in letting yourself feel joy because you are afraid of the letdown. Instead, experience the elation and excitement of being on the mountaintop. In addition, write down those highs and victories so that you can reflect on them when you are in the valley.

Speaking of valleys...yes they will happen. Sometimes you may feel you are experiencing many more defeats than victories. It's in these times when allowing yourself to feel the disappointment, frustration, anger or sadness associated with the lows is important. No one likes to feel sad or disappointed, but it is going to happen. People will let you down and hurt you. Heartfelt prayers said with a pure heart may go unanswered at times. Allow yourself to cry, and ride the lows. If you repress those emotions, they will not stay down for long, and you will have a much larger mess on your hands. Crying and releasing those emotions is a vehicle for healing and resolution.

When you get on a roller coaster at an amusement park, you don't get to pick the part of the ride you want to be on. Instead, once you are buckled in and the ride begins, you can't get off in the middle or before the scary parts begin. Instead, you have to ride the ride until it comes a complete stop. The same concept applies to church planting. We don't get to choose many of the parts of the ride in church planting, but God holds onto us like a harness on a roller coaster, and in His arms we can find safety no matter if we riding high, or sinking low.

Persevere

I have both heard and read that the key to successful church planting is perseverance. Church planting has been compared multiple times to a marathon, rather than a sprint, and yet sprinting is much easier than running a marathon.

When I was in middle school, I ran track. My coach tried to put me in a long distance run, but I was horrible at it. I am all of 5'2 and a half, and my short little legs had difficulty going long distances. A few weeks into the track season, the coach asked me to try sprint running, which I agreed to. Surprisingly, I found my niche. My favorite race was the 50-yard dash because even though it was hard on my body to run as fast and as hard as I could, it was over within a couple of minutes. The pain and discomfort didn't last long, and it was an easy race to recover from. I was quite successful as a sprinter and earned several medals and ribbons.

One day, a girl on my track team became sick, and my coach asked me to take her place in the 440-yard relay race. My heart sank as I thought about running all the way around the track at a sprint, rather than running my normal short sprint of 50 yards. I reluctantly agreed to run the race, and as the gun shot I bolted out of the starting line. I was feeling good until I passed my usual 50 yards. Suddenly, I became short of breath, my heart raced, and I just wanted to collapse.

My coach, who knew I would hit a wall after that 50-yard mark was right there to cheer me on. She kept yelling, "Go Angie." You can do it. Persevere!" I finished my part and handed the baton off just in time for the next runner to take off. Even though I was tired, I felt so proud of myself for persevering and finishing the race.

In church planting, we typically bolt off the starting line with energy and passion. As time passes though, we become short of breath as we ride the highs and lows. On the roller coaster of church planting, we hit walls and discouragement sets in, making us want to quit.

If you're like most church planters and their wives, you probably want to quit your church every week. Sundays can be the most depressing and discouraging days of the week. Emotions run high on Sundays and Mondays, following either a great Sunday, or a not so great Sunday. We can be tempted to make choices and decisions out of emotion, yet decisions made when we are in a high emotional state are rarely wise ones.

During times of emotion, we are very vulnerable, and the enemy takes full advantage to whisper lies, and worm his way into our thought processes. He may whisper such lies as, *"you deserve better,"* or *"this isn't even worth it, you might as well just quit."* Recognize those voices as out and out deception and take those thoughts captive while remembering that your journey of church planting requires determination and perseverance.

1 Timothy 4:7 says, *"I have fought the good fight, I have finished the race, I have kept the faith"* (NIV). This verse speaks very specifically to the concept of perseverance and the required fight to keep on keeping on.

Planting a church is not a sprint, but requires determination and fight. When you want to quit, when you want to give up, lift your eyes to Jesus, your own personal track coach for cheerleading and encouragement. He will be there to help you keep that faith and persevere.

Remain Teachable

My Mother is a strong woman of faith and imparted many nuggets of wisdom to me. As a child, when I got into trouble my Mom disciplined me, and then asked me what I needed to learn from the situation. To complete the process of the discipline method my Mom implemented, I was required to tell her what I learned, and what I planned to do differently moving forward. Even though my Mom's method drove me crazy at the time, she engrained a wise truth in me that I still carry today. This method has served me well.

Whether you are on the mountaintop or in the deep valley of despair in your journey of church planting, God wants you to remain teachable. Sometimes God uses our circumstances to discipline us and asks us the question my Mom asked of me, which is, *"what do you need to learn?"*

A year and a half in our journey of church planting, my dear friend Rita, who is a Lead Pastor's wife asked me how I was enjoying church planting, and being a Lead Pastor's wife. I laughed and told her that we knew everything about church planting, and leading a church until... we actually had to do it. I went on to tell her that God had used our experiences to teach us many hard life lessons. She smiled and kindly told me to *"stay teachable,"* because God will always honor humility and a teachable heart.

Psalm 94:12-13 says, *"Blessed is the man whom You discipline and instruct, O Lord, and teach out of your law you may give him power to keep himself calm in the days of adver sity, until the pit of destruction is dug for the wicked"* (NIV). This verse is rich with wisdom and promise that God blesses and honors us when we submit to His discipline, and what He desires to teach us. As you ride the roller coaster of church planting, do not forget to stop during times of adversity or hardship and ask God what He desires to teach you. Be careful not to spin your wheels pointing your finger in blame, and allowing bitterness to creep in, but be humble and allow God to instruct and teach you.

As you seek to be teachable on your own personal roller coaster, you may be tempted to look at all of the mistakes and failures you made. It is important to evaluate where we went wrong, but focusing too much on our failures can inevitably send us to a pit of despair and into a valley. Instead, focus on the "what now," concept.

In her book, "I Dare You," Joyce Meyer says, *"There is nothing you can do about what has already been done—but you can do something about how you respond.".* [7]

Our responses during times of discipline and teaching are crucial and set the stage for what happens next. We can either spin in our failures and get nowhere, or we can look ahead and respond with humility and an open heart to God, which will take us to a place of restoration. He will shed light on those areas He is seeking to refine in you, and will ride that coaster with you as He teaches you His ways.

Do Not Look to the Right or the Left-- Look Ahead

---

[7] Meyer, Joyce, I Dare You. Embrace Life With Passion (New York, NY: FaithWords, 2007). Pg. 133.

I addressed the issue of comparing in chapter 4, titled "The Dangerous Game of Comparing," but wanted to touch on the issue again in this section.

Many of the stories we hear in church planting are the huge success stories; the churches that grew exponentially in a short span of time. These stories can serve to build our faith, but they can also serve to discourage us, especially if our church plant does not measure up to the *so-called* standard.

It is normal to look to the right and left as we navigate the roller coaster of church planting. We may ride high when we know that our church plant is doing better than someone else's. On the other hand, we may quickly sink low when we read about a church plant far exceeding what our church plant is doing. Looking to the right and left instead of ahead will kill your momentum and motivation more quickly than anything else. I have been guilty of this trap many times.

A church that meets in a theater (like our church) is located in a town just 20 miles south of us. The pastor is a phenomenal leader and under his leadership the church grew very quickly, and in a short amount of time. Some days I cannot help but compare where we are at numerically and financially to that church. It never fails that when I look down that path, the result is that I get discouraged and want to quit. Comparing your church to other churches is easy to do though, especially when others around you also make comparisons.

On the other hand, there is another church in that same town that has been around for seven years, and they average lower attendance, than our church plant does. It would make sense that comparing our church plant to the one that is by some people's standards," not doing as well as ours," would serve to elevate me or make me feel better. Quite the contrary! Instead, I struggle with being proud and lazy and comparing makes me want to stick with the status quo instead of pressing on to be better and do more for God.

The bottom line is, looking around you to what other church plants are doing is dangerous and tricky. There is nothing wrong with swapping ideas with other planters or asking their advice on how to get over the humps, however if your intention is to compare, watch out.

Looking to the left and to the right, instead of focusing on your mission and calling will distract you and deplete you. Those other church plants are reaching people you cannot reach, and your church plant is reaching people they cannot reach. Remain focused on what God called you to do in your church plant. Fix your eyes ahead and above, and stayed committed to the vision and mission God gave you and your husband for your city.

Recently, I went back and read the story of Lot's wife found in Genesis 19:1-26. Angels escorted Lot's family out of Sodom and Gomorrah as God rained down fire and destroyed the city. The angels specifically commanded Lot and his family to flee the city and not look back. We know too well what happened to Lot's wife who turned into a pillar of salt as she looked back instead of ahead.

This example serves to remind us to keep our eyes on Christ and the mission He called us to accomplish. When we look to the right and to the left, we become *salty* with resentment, frustration, and entitlement. God may have performed an amazing miracle the day before, but as we look at what He did for another church plant, seeds of entitlement take root as we believe that we deserve more. This sense of entitlement will do nothing more than destroy you, and hinders God's blessing in your life.

God has called you and your husband to something unique and special that only you can accomplish because of your own unique gifts and talents. Focus on that, and stay away from the trap of comparing. In doing so, your roller coaster ride will be more thrilling and exciting as God takes you up and over the highs and lows of the journey of church planting.

Part III

Oh The Places You Will Go!

> I can't imagine anything
> more worthwhile than
> doing what I most love.
> And they pay me for it.
> ~Edgar Winter~

CHAPTER 9

You Want Me To Do What?
Differentiating Between God's Call and Obligation

I often talk to my husband Jon about my struggle with making choices out of obligation and guilt, rather than a true desire to do something. It is a messed up way to live life, and church planting hasn't helped one bit with my struggle. In the world of church planting there are tasks that constantly need to be done, and many of these tasks are not ones that people readily step up to do. When I hear of a need in our church, I immediately want to figure out how I can fill the need. The problem is that many times, I step up to fill the need out of obligation, rather than out of desire. I am by nature a fixer, and so I naturally want to solve the problem.

I know that many planter wives relate to this struggle and also readily step up to fill needs in their church plants. This is a quality I love about planter wives, as most are hard workers with a desire to serve. God has certainly called us to deny ourselves, and put others first, but where is the balance? Are you fulfilling God's specific call on your life, or are you serving out of obligation?

What Has God Called Me To, Anyway?

One of the most common musings I have heard from planter wives is the difficulty with figuring out their role or place in the church plant. Some planter wives serve as a co-pastor and work alongside their husbands in a highly involved capacity in the church. Other planter wives prefer to be more in the background and "plug holes" as needed in areas of the church where no one else is serving.

There is a broad range of involvement available to planter wives, but many times a wife may find herself knowing what the *church* has called her to achieve, but is left wondering what *God* has called her to accomplish.

Sometimes God and the church plant are so intertwined that it can be difficult to differentiate between the two. We established in previous chapters that planter wives are a group of women who work hard and rise to the tasks asked of them in a heartbeat. Honestly though, these tasks we rise to can often be out of obligation and necessity rather than passion and a fulfillment of the call God has on our lives, which can leave planter wives with emptiness and resentment.

So what should a planter wife do when a need arises in the church plant and she feels obligated fill the need?

The Danger of Saying Yes out of Obligation

Three weeks before the launch of our church, a couple leading our Children's department stepped out and moved to another ministry position. Children's ministry is so crucial to the success of a church, so the hole had to be filled quickly, but there was no budget to hire someone who was qualified to run a children's department. I saw the stress and worry on my husband's face as he looked at the looming launch date, and at the very huge hole that needed to be filled.

At that moment, I was faced with a choice. I could either step in "for such a time as this," or I could just hope and pray that God would send someone else to do the job. To be quite honest, Children's ministry is not my forte. Nothing makes me feel more anxiety and stress than a room full of loud, children. Yet there was a big need, and I felt obligated to volunteer for the job. I took a deep breath and told my husband I would step in to direct the kids department. He looked at me with both horror and relief, but he really did not have time to question my reasons.

The next few weeks were a whirlwind, and there were many tears, and stress filled days as I tried my best to step out of my comfort zone, and lead a major department in our church. Our church launched and it felt like there were a thousand screaming kids running around. Thank goodness for amazing volunteers who actually do have a heart for kids because if it was not for them, I probably would have lost my mind.

Week after week, I led the Kids department and hated every minute of it. I was empty, felt taken advantage of, and frustrated because I knew that God most certainly did NOT call me to be a Children's Director. The truth is; I stunk at it!

One Sunday, everything came to a head as Jon and I fought about this issue of my "having to be the kid's director." Enough was enough and he decided step out in faith and hire someone. Sweeter words could not have been spoken that day as relief washed over me. I actually jumped up and down and shouted, "thank God" the day our new children's director took over.

I learned some hard lessons during that season, but the biggest lesson is that I should **NEVER** say yes to a task out of obligation. Although it is tempting to say yes out of obligation, we should instead take the time to pray about the situation so that we can differentiate between God's call, and obligation, because there's a big difference!

Dealing With the Expectations of People

I am always amazed at the expectations people place on church planter wives. It is unfair and yet many people automatically expect a church planter's wife to say yes to everything asked of her, **and** provide service with a smile. Even though as church planters we have the opportunity to cultivate a culture where, we teach people realistic expectations, unrealistic expectations of both the planter and his wife will inevitably creep in.

In the beginning stages of a church plant, it is easy to fall into a trap of pleasing people. The truth is, you need people on your team to help launch a church and so seeking to please people, and keep them happy is something that all church planters deal with. The problem with this mindset is that unrealistic and unfair expectations can be put into place by people in your church leaving you empty and depleted because no one can please all the people all the time.

There some practical ways to handle and deal with the expectations of others so that you do not completely lose your mind, and sight of what God has called you to do.

Become Comfortable With Your Own Limitations

That is right, my friend you have limitations and there is nothing wrong with that. There is only so much one person can do and when we have too many tasks piled on our plate, nothing gets accomplished with excellence. If you work outside the home in addition to being a church planter wife, this concept is of particular importance.

One of my friends who is a planter wife, is also a teacher, and puts in 40-50 hours a week at her job. Some people in her church expected her to attend every event and coordinate women's ministries. She did so out of obligation but soon began to experience burn-out. Finally, she realized that she had way exceeded her limits and began to delegate some of the ministries she was tasked with. In the end, God sent other leaders and she soon replenished, as she surrendered to her limitations.

Call Out Expectations

Call out the expectations and deal with them. If someone in your church voices an expectation of you, this might be the perfect opportunity for you to discuss the expectation with that person. I realize that conflict is no fun and most wives would rather just do the task and rise to the expectations of others, rather than set a boundary. However, we teach others how to treat us and one positive aspect of church planting is that as wives we set the stage for how people in the church treat both us and staff members' wives.

We had a woman on our launch team who was a real go-getter but she often voiced her expectations of me, and to be quite honest they were way outside the realm of reality. I fell into the trap of trying to please her because she was such an asset to our team and I was afraid that if I let her down, she would leave. This pattern lasted for several months until it dawned on me that as long as I continued to submit to her expectations, the bar would go higher and higher, and she would never be satisfied.

I had to do something and after seeking God for help, the door to *call out the expectation* swung wide open one day. The woman informed me that as the pastor's wife I should meet with women from our church every day for lunch or coffee, despite working full-time and having a family to care for. I have to admit that frustration helped fuel my confidence as I informed her that her expectation of me was unrealistic, and that I was not going to sacrifice my family or personal mental health. She became irritated with me until I asked her in a gentle way how her family would feel if she missed dinner and activities every night so that she could have meetings. Suddenly, her whole countenance changed as she put into perspective what I said. That day changed everything and from then on out the woman was much more respectful of me, and my time when she asked something of me. Who knew simply calling the expectation out in the open could open such a door for change?

Say It With Me--No.

Go ahead, say it....**No**. Perhaps you just needed someone to give you permission to use a word that many church planters' wives avoid because when they do say **no**, they experience immense guilt. Guilt is an intense emotion that can steer us in the wrong direction and when we respond or react out of guilt our choices are usually not wise ones.

Most planter wives feel overwhelmed. Usually, there is much more work than there are workers, and because we love our church plant and our husband, we often find ourselves saying yes when our hearts are screaming **NO!**

This issue of not saying no is probably one you have struggled with and may continue to struggle with unless you learn to appropriately deal with the ensuing feelings of guilt that accompany the word no.

In order stay healthy and ward off feelings of resentment you must learn to say no. If you have feelings of guilt when you say no to something, stop, and pray about whether or not the guilt you have is healthy guilt, or unhealthy guilt.

Healthy guilt is conviction of the Holy Spirit and happens when He is trying to get our attention. Unhealthy guilt is followed by shame, which is not from God. Unhealthy guilt sends us the message of, "*if you were a good Pastor's wife, or really loved God, you wouldn't say no.*" In the few seconds you have to respond after you are presented a task, ask the Holy Spirit for wisdom on how to respond.

The word **no** is not a curse word and needs to be a part of our vocabulary. Learn to deal with feelings of guilt and determine if what you feel is healthy guilt or unhealthy guilt. Saying no may take practice on your part, but try it. You will feel lighter from the burden of obligation, and in return God could use your **no** to be someone else's **yes**.

Saying Yes Out of Obligation
Robs You and Others

Earlier in this chapter I shared a big failure of mine when I said yes to lead the kids department at our church out of obligation rather than out of God's call. I simply did not trust Him and that He would send the right person to lead that department, but instead took on the task myself. I was prideful, and in the end my lack of faith robbed me, and our church of God's best.

God does not need us, but instead He chooses to use us to accomplish His plan. God sees your BIG heart and desire to rise to the challenge and say yes to anything asked of you, but God also desires to call others to accomplish tasks for Him.

Saying yes out of obligation not only robs you, but it also robs other people. When we say yes out of plain obligation it is almost as if we tell God, we do not trust Him enough to send someone else to do the task. Many times God is also working on other people to do things for Him and they just may be ready to say yes if we say no.

In my situation with the Kids department there was an amazing leader waiting in the wings the whole time. This lady volunteered in our Kids department and was top notch. She was highly organized and had a passion for children. I later discovered, after many miserable months in the kids area that she would have been happy to step up and coordinate our Children's department. If I had just had faith in God and let Him open the door, rather than saying yes out of obligation, I could have saved myself and my husband a lot of frustration. My lack of of faith and inability to say no robbed me in that I spent five months stressed, and on the brink of a mental breakdown. It also robbed this lady because she could not use her gift in full capacity.

Thank goodness for God's patience and grace! Saying no and choosing not to accept a task out of obligation opens the door for God to use people you would never expect, to do what you never could.

Food For Thought

Perhaps you are chewing on this concept of differentiating between what God's call and obligation. As you reflect on your choices think about why you have a problem saying no. Is it out of guilt? Are you a fixer? Are you allowing the expectations of others drive your decisions?

My mentor and friend, Mary Beth Bradshaw provided profound wisdom on this topic. She said,

"Philippians says "I CAN do all things through Christ who gives me strength." It doesn't say you HAVE to DO all things. As a church planter and wife we fall into the trap of this; of doing it all and then burn out or break down. Ask the LORD for guidance as to what is important and vital to your ministry and then set aside those things that are not... and don't feel GUILTY about NOT doing it." Well said, Mary Beth.

I encourage and challenge you to pray about this struggle. Ask God to help you decipher between when to say yes and when to say no. Learn to be comfortable with your particular limitations and pray about those opportunities God may bring your way to *call out* unrealistic expectations people place on you.

Keep in mind that God just might have someone else in mind for a task and that if you say no, it just might open the door for someone else to say yes.

> "You're off to Great Places!
> Today is your day!
> Your mountain is waiting,
> So... get on your way!"
> — **Dr. Seuss (Oh, the Places You'll Go!)**

CHAPTER 10

I Never Knew I Could Do That!
God can use you in ways you NEVER dreamed.

Once upon a time there was a young, beautiful woman who possessed grace and poise. She was an unpretentious girl who envisioned a life much like her ancestors; a life of tradition and simplicity. The girl lived a predictable life and was content with the daily tasks she carried out until one day; an event occurred that changed her destiny forever. Her life was never the same and yet the girl whose faith in God was strong chose to follow a call, and as a result of her obedience, a nation was changed forever.

You have probably figured out the woman described is Esther, found in the book of Esther in the Bible. The life of Esther has been used countless times in conjunction with themes at conferences or books that call people for *"such a time as this,"* to accomplish great things for God. It is much easier to read about a character in the Bible or see a hero on television accomplish the impossible, than it is to envision such greatness in our own lives. Most people do not see themselves as someone who will accomplish the extraordinary, or even anything of significance. It is extremely difficult to make the connection that God could ever use little ole' me to do anything like the heroes of faith we read about in the Bible.

As daughters of the King, God gave to us the same inheritance as the heroes we read about in the Bible. In fact, we have opportunities provided to us people of the Bible never had such as technology, the ability to travel long distances in a short amount of time, smart phones, etc. to accomplish much for God.

As a church planter's wife you have numerous opportunities available to you to be creative and start new ministries simply because the church is new. There is no previous pastor's wife or previous way of doing things so the opportunities are limitless!

So what will you do with those opportunities? Will you, like Esther trust God for such a time as this? I hope so; because when faith, trust in God and a willing heart combine they are an unstoppable force. I am confident that if you take hold of God's desire to work in and through you, He will use you in ways you never even dreamed.

Church Planter Wives are Amazing

I love spending time with other church planter wives. If you don't have a network of church planter wives, I highly encourage you to surround yourself with other like-minded women on the same journey as you. You can read more about how to develop a network of planter wives in chapter 14, *"The Importance of Relationships."*

When I hang out with other church planter wives, I am simply amazed at what they accomplish. Their stories challenge me, encourage me, and motivate me to do more. I believe that God gives planter wives incredible abilities, and opens doors to accomplish things because of their obedience and willing hearts. Just like, Esther planter wives have chosen to trust and obey their God and He in turn has anointed them in ways many women never experience. The favor of God rests on planter wives and infuses them with energy, strength, creativity, and fervor.

It is an honor to be a planter's wife. Think about that concept for a moment. Perhaps you have never viewed your role as a planter wife as an honor before.

When I was a youth pastor's wife I had the privilege of serving with a very wise Senior Pastor's wife named Sue. Sue was a quiet, humble, sweet person who spoke a nugget of wisdom I have never forgotten. In a setting with the staff wives, she discussed what an honor and privilege it is to be a pastor's wife because we are automatically provided with a platform to influence and speak into other people's lives. She went on to say that most people would give their left arm to have such influence and yet God trusted us with that platform simply because we are pastor's wives. From that day forward, I never viewed my role as a woman, and pastor's wife the same way.

God has given you a platform and a place of influence

just like He did Esther. He desires for you to know that you are simply amazing and that your potential is huge. Today Jesus wants you to know His favor and blessing is on you, and that He desires to use you to blaze trails of glory for Him. God knows you are amazing, I know you are amazing, but do you know you are simply amazing?

What Is Stopping You?

I recently spoke at a women's retreat about the concept of influence, and how God desires to use women to influence and impact the world around them.

One night I spoke about the labels we carry that are negative, and how these labels serve as obstacles that prevent us from carrying out the call of God in our lives. I had the women quickly write down five labels on a piece of paper and asked them to think about the *purpose* the labels had in their lives. That night, God moved in powerful ways, and freed women from the labels given to them by other people and by themselves.

I know I have struggled for years with labels. I grew up very poor and always felt like I was not as good as other people. My father never told me he was proud of me and often told me he felt sorry for my future husband. For years I carried labels such as *worthless, insignificant, poor girl, failure,* and these labels stopped me from pursuing dreams God placed in my heart.

I continued to struggle with my labels, but a few years ago God brought me to a crossroads and asked which road I was going to take. I had two choices. I could continue to walk down the path and let the labels dictate my life, or I could walk in freedom and choose to believe what Jesus said about me. Church planting is what brought me to that crossroads because I could no longer hide. God had chosen me to be a church planter's wife and to do great things for Him. Just like Esther, I had to choose; so I did. I chose God's path and shook off those labels.

Perhaps you have labels you struggle with. I challenge you to write down some of those labels and take time to think about the labels you wrote down.

Ask yourself these questions: How do I live my life out of these labels? How do these labels serve as obstacles to accomplish what God has asked of me? Perhaps today God is bringing you to a cross roads and asking you the same question He asked me.

Psalm 119:32 says, *"I run in the path of your commands, for you have set my heart free"* (NIV). God wants to set you free of labels and He desires to help you shake off those labels and instead give you new ones. Will you let Him?

I Have a Dream

When I was a little girl, I watched a television show where a girl ran around in circles with her arms out and eventually took off, flying through the air. After watching the show, I ran outside and began running around in circles with my arms out, knowing that any second I too would lift off and fly through the air. I envisioned myself soaring over my house through the clouds, just like the little girl on television did. I did not fly, but instead became tired and out of breath. My older sister soon informed me that my dream to fly was stupid and pointless, which gave me my first dose of disappointment about dreams. From that point on, my whole perspective about dreams and my abilities was tainted. When I had dreams or ideas, I immediately thought of all the reasons I would never accomplish the goal.

Maybe you can relate. Perhaps you have dreams that have lay dormant for years and put those dreams on a shelf because of your own reasoning process. Maybe as a child someone doused your flame, and you vowed to never dream again so that you did not experience the sting of disappointment. If so this section was written specifically for you!

God designed us with a desire to dream. He placed dreams in you for the specific purpose of bringing glory to Him and drawing others into relationship with their Creator. Planting a church provides a wide open gateway where the dreams and desires God placed in you can be accomplished.

But how do we overcome past disappointment and failure to dream again? The simple answer is that you just do. I have written enough about my own failures to let you know that I have struggled with this concept several times in my life. It seems like a never-ending pattern that goes something like this. I have a dream, I fail, I quit, God picks me up and I try again. Repeat.

When you dream, you will fail, and you will be disappointed. You will want to quit, but do not give up! Now is the time to dust off those dreams, or this could be the perfect time to dream new dreams.

Maybe you have always envisioned running a group for young Moms. Perhaps you have creative ways to reach out to women in your community. Take time daily to pray about those dreams and ideas God has given you. He will be faithful to provide open doors and motivation for you to accomplish those dreams. Church planting provides a blank canvas for you to live out those dreams God gave you for the express purpose of ministering to others. In the midst of those dreams becoming reality, you will experience favor and blessing from God as well as contentment in knowing that your dreams are coming true. Despite past disappointment or failure, dust yourself off, and dream. What does God want to do through your dreams?

A Little Inspiration from other Church Planter Wives

Most of us enjoy reading inspirational stories. Church planter wives inspire me more than anyone else and I love to hear about ways they are living out the dreams God gave them. I hope you enjoy reading how other planter wives are dreaming big dreams for God and how He is using them in amazing ways.

Renee Exley – Life Church – Midlothian, Texas

We had a dream of reaching those who have been hurt in church or those who said they would never step foot in a church because of past hurts caused by "Christians." We also wanted to reach the "d-church" generation. With these two populations combined they make up 40% of our church! We knew it was going to take us being real and transparent as well. We also went out in our community, lived life there, did outreaches to them, loved them and now they are seeing the real Love.

Another dream I have is to see women reaching across generations to mentor and be around them.

Chasity Ross – Brighton, CO

I had a dream of seeing the women in our church come together to reach the un-churched and lost women in their circles of influence around them, their work, their neighborhoods, their communities, etc. We get together once a month and do something fun, not churchy, but something an unbeliever would want to come to. This opens up a door to show Christ's love to them. To care for them right where they were at. It gave us opportunities to share our lives with them and our struggles and share how Jesus helped us to overcome. They see we are real women who hurt like they do and we too have messy lives and we can't get it together all the time, but Jesus is who we hold fast too, to trust Him with my mess, to redeem me, to love me, to make me new, to forgive me.

Amber Woller – Corner Church – Minneapolis, MN

We had a dream of owning a coffee shop that was open to the community during the week with church services held on Sunday. The idea was to use the coffee shop to build relationships in a non-threatening environment.

We began renting a coffee shop to hold our weekly service while looking for a place to start our own shop. The owners of the shop we met in, approached us a year after meeting there and asked if we wanted to buy their shop. It was chaotic and messy becoming coffee shop owners, but we daily get to be a part of our community. Many customers have no clue that a church owns the coffee shop, but they often say that something is different about our place. Although we don't have any amazing life-changing stories yet to come out of our coffee shop, we have know we are planting seeds that will one day emerge as beautiful plants. One customer who was desperately seeking began coming to church. She considers the church her family even though she still has not grasped the full truth of Jesus. She moved away a few months ago but still keeps in touch. We continue to pray for her and other customers like her.

Allison Crum – High Calling Church – Eastpoint, FL

Our Church, High Calling Church is committed to revealing the saving grace and restorative mercy of Jesus to the community. We are doing this by preaching the cross of Christ and ministering to the needs of individuals through the gifts of the Spirit. We are evangelizing the disconnected and teaching believers by leading them through a discipleship pathway and enabling them to minister and meet the needs of those around them both inside and outside the church walls. It is the desire of High Calling Church to be a place where everyone has a purpose in God's plan.

Your "Such a Time as This"

So, what has God called you to for such a time as this? The possibilities are endless, so dream big dreams for God and watch as He uses you in ways you never thought possible. I encourage you to grab a notebook, sit quiet before the Lord and listen. Be ready to write down the dreams He gives you. Then, pray for God to open doors and equip you to fulfill those dreams. Like Esther, your life will never be the same and as you walk in submission and obedience to the Lord, He will use you in ways you never dreamed.

Reflection Questions

1. How have disappointments kept you from pursuing your dreams?

    _____

    _____

    _____

2. Write down five labels you have that stop you from pursuing your dreams?

    _____

    _____

    _____

3. Take a moment and pray about dreams that God is calling you to pursue. Write down your dreams and ask for God to open the doors for these dreams to become reality.

    _____

    _____

    _____

Use this page to continue to write down dreams God has placed in your heart. Journal and jot down some ideas.

> All the world is made of
> faith, and trust,
> and pixie dust."
> — **J.M. Barrie (Peter Pan)**

CHAPTER 11

Just A Little Pixie Dust
Along with Faith and Hard Work

In my work as a therapist, I encounter people who are in their greatest time of need. The clients in my practice who seek out counseling are in pain, and are desperately seeking the right formula or solution to get out of that pain. I often tell my clients that although I wish I had a magic wand or pixie dust available that could make all of their problems disappear; the reality is that anything worthwhile requires hard work and faith in God. I also encourage them that although the journey back to health and wholeness is difficult, what they discover about themselves and God is well worth the hard work necessary to accomplish the goals they set.

An Honest Question

This same concept of the need for faith and hard work also applies to church planting. Most church planters are by nature, hard working people who stand ready to dig in and extend every effort necessary to plant a church. Church planter wives are no exception. The work ethic of planter wives is astounding and because of their tenacity and perseverance, they are a huge asset to the success of the church. If church planters were simply looking for an easy type of career or task, they probably wouldn't have chosen to plant a church.

So, how then do we as church planters and wives make the leap from the **knowledge** that planting a church will require faith in God and hard work, to an **expectation** that a magical sequence of events will occur that will make the church an instant success?

When my husband and I started the church planting process we read every book available and researched models of church planting in a grand search for just the right formula that would make our church successful. To be honest, I believe what we really wanted was a little pixie dust to sprinkle, or a magic wand to wave so that **"poof"** we had instant success.

God is certainly a God of miracles and we have seen Him perform many; however God is also a God who requires us to work hard, and to be faithful with what He has entrusted to us, even when our church isn't always **magical.**

In our constant pursuit of magic, the potential for burnout and weariness strongly exists and causes us to want to quit altogether.

Becoming Weary Can Equal Death

Sadly, there are many planters who become "weary in doing good," and do not get the opportunity to reap the harvest.

The town we planted in (Parker, Colorado) is fondly nicknamed by the local pastors as a *"church planter's graveyard."* The reason is because numerous church plants have come and gone. A local pastor in our town who we met with before starting our church informed us that he had seen so many church plants open and close, that he had lost count. We were sobered at this information and were desperate to know how we could avoid being one of those statistics. Jon and I spent the next couple of hours picking this Pastor's brain, asking question after question about how **NOT** to be another one of those dead church plants. This seasoned Pastor was kind enough to give us a nugget of wisdom that we have carried since that meeting several years ago. He said, you must *"have faith, work hard and stick with it!"*

Now this nugget of wisdom sounds simple enough but when the going gets rough, our natural instinct is *fight or flight*. We either want to stay and work or we want to run to something more comfortable. Here's where the true rubber meets the road and we have the choice to either have faith in God or run.

The pastor I spoke of is a man of integrity and character and as we continued to talk, he shared his story with us. This Pastor had come to an established church that had a building, but was in financial trouble and had a brewing moral scandal the last Pastor had ignored. The first three-plus years of his itineration as Pastor were met with struggles, and he admitted that he was not the popular pastor. He shared about how he pleaded with God to let him leave the church because it was just too hard, but God continually told him to have faith and work hard. His hard work and faith in God paid off. Six years into his pastorate, the church is a thriving and growing healthy church that is now running two services. Perhaps he found a secret formula for success? Probably not, because his journey did not consist of any "secret formula," but instead, required constant dependence on God and faith that He was in control of a very difficult situation. The result of his hard work and faith in God resulted in a harvest of a healthy church and many coming to Christ.

Stories like this one are reminders NOT to give up in difficult times. Yet there are times when we may ask ourselves if what we are doing is even worth it.

This Just Isn't Worth It

The Lord has dealt with me swiftly on this very issue time and time again. I have been guilty of anger and frustration toward both God and our church because the road has been difficult. I cannot even count how many Sundays I have told Jon we should just quit because this task is just too hard. We've asked the same questions over and over, week after week, month after month and yet many times we are met with silence from God.

It seems that each week brings the same broken record of questions. "Why can't people just give so we can make budget?" "Why can't God just provide so we can get a paycheck?" "Are we ever going to have health insurance?" "Why can't people just be faithful with church attendance?"

Does my whiny little, poor me song sound familiar?

I am guilty of pitching my hissy fits in an attempt to get God's attention. When I feel His silence and perceive it as Him ignoring me, I act just like a toddler and throw myself on the ground, kicking and screaming. Yet in the midst of my fit, God quietly waits until I calm down so that He can reassure me that He is in control and that I simply need to have faith in Him.

Sometimes, faith is not so simple. I wonder if you can relate. I am not on a quest to place a guilt trip on anyone and I believe that church planter wives are faith-filled women of God who believe in what God has called them and their husbands to do. However, along the road when you have dodged curve balls and navigated trials so intense and difficult that your faith has been zapped and feels shriveled up, worked so hard that you're exhausted, it's in these times that a little *pixie dust* could go a long way. One such area of testing that many planter wives struggle with and one that threatens our faith and resilience is the lack of security and stability that exists in church planting.

No Stability of Security? Sign Me UP!

God is aware of our need for stability and a sense of security and yet church planting steals any sense of security and stability away from us. It is a harsh statement, but it is true. The safety and security you knew probably went right out the door the moment you said yes to the call of church planting. I know it did for me.

We went from a nice salary with benefits and comfort to a very small salary, no health insurance and a constant worry about how we would make ends meet. There have been months when had to go to our town's local food bank just to put food on the table. Many times, we have sold items just to pay utilities and put gas in the car. I have had many conversations with other planter wives who report the same things. This task God has called you and your husband to, is no easy one and the sacrifice you make as a women is significant. I have often pondered why God made me as a woman with such a need for stability and security, but called me and my husband to do something where there is very little stability and security. You may have asked the same question.

So, how then do we navigate our need for stability and security with the reality that the charge of planting a church that we have been tasked with does NOT have the ability to meet these needs?

A Gentle Reminder

One of my favorite scriptures comes from Ephesians 6:9 which says, *"Let us not become weary in doing good, for at the proper time we will reap a harvest if we do not give up."* *(NIV)* This scripture reassures me to keep, keeping on. I can almost hear Paul cheering on the sidelines saying, "Keep going!" "Work Hard!" "Have Faith!"

Just this little bit of encouragement serves as a little *pixie dust* to keep us on the right path. In addition, God is so faithful to also send others to encourage and cheerlead or remind us of how we have impacted them. These gentle reminders are just a glimpse of a harvest that requires hard work and faith, and yet is so fulfilling that nothing else could replace the feeling of God's favor when we obey Him. Along with a much needed boost in faith, this scripture is a reminder from the Lord that our need for security and stability can never be met by a nice, fat paycheck. God is the only one who can fill our need for stability and security. Quite simply, we have **ALL** we need in Him.

How then do we keep this perspective when we are

weary and our faith tanks are on empty?

The Moses Challenge

About a year into our church plant, The Lord led me to study the life of Moses. Moses was an amazing man of God and served as a Pastor to people who saw miracle after miracle yet grumbled against God. The people questioned God and Moses on a regular basis and what Moses had to endure would have probably made most of us resign after the first week. Interestingly enough there were times when God wanted to destroy the Israelites and yet Moses begged for God's mercy on their behalf.

As I studied the life of Moses, my overwhelming reaction was two-fold. *First*, I longed to be faithful and wholly trust God, like Moses did. *Second*, I felt frustration and conflict because Moses worked hard, trusted God and yet his pastorate was more difficult and trying than anyone could imagine. Poor Moses didn't even get to reap his harvest and enter the Promised Land, due to the disobedience of the people he led.

The conflict I felt continued to be ignited as I looked at how hard Jon and I worked to plant our church. I mean it should be simple, right? Obey God, work hard, trust Him, and reap a harvest. Repeat. Yet, as I look at great men of God, my way of thinking just does not fit into the simple little notch in the ways I think it should.

Moses, Joshua, Caleb, Elijah, Paul and many more followed God with reckless abandon. They worked hard, trusted God, and obeyed Him at every turn and yet many times their ministries were met with hardship, sacrifice and difficulty that required an even stronger dependence on God. So often, they did not get to see that harvest but they never gave up, and continued to do well in the eyes of the Lord.

Why do we feel that if the magic isn't there, or the sacrifice is too great, that it is okay to throw in the towel and give up? My heart hurts as I write this because I have said the words countless times, *"I just give up; this isn't worth it."*

I Am Not Anything Like--Them

It is easy to lose faith and want to give up. In my study of Moses, I often found myself exacerbated by the wishy-washy attitude the Israelites displayed. God performed incredible miracles for them, and yet their faith in God seemed to vanish in a matter of minutes as they then looked at the next issue to complain and grumble about.

How many times are we are just like, The Israelites? If we sat down and listed all of the miracles God has done for us, we probably could not even recall the many times He provided for needs or answered prayers we uttered in complete desperation. I wonder how differently the story in Exodus would have been if only The Israelites had truly trusted *their* God. I wonder how differently our stories would be if we truly trusted *our* God?

A Faith Filled Challenge

My good friend Mindy has been kind enough to listen to many of my complaining tangents and one day after several minutes of sitting silent on the phone while I rambled on and on about how difficult life was, she gently encouraged me to sit down and make a list of all of the prayers God had answered in the last few months. I was a bit irritated at her because I simply wanted to continue in my mode of complaining. Just call me an Israelite!

After we hung up, I sat down with a notebook and a pen and took her challenge. I was soon humbled as I filled several pages with miracles, and answered prayers. This simple exercise served the purpose of catapulting me out of my misery and into a brand new faith-filled perspective.

I challenge you to also sit down and list all of the miracles God has done for you. I promise you that this exercise will build your faith and carry you through even the driest, desert experience.

A Small Shift in Perspective

Many times we do not need the earth to move in order to have our faith lifted. Sometimes, just a small change in life serves to provide a fresh perspective and renewed motivation. If circumstances are difficult in your church plant it does not mean that you are outside of God's will. It does not mean that you and your husband made a mistake in planting a church. It does not mean that God is not pleased with you. Yes, we must always examine what we do and pray about what we are trying to accomplish.

Most church planters have pure hearts and a longing to see people come to Christ. They have chased a God-sized dream hand-in-hand with their spouses and yet get sucked into the Bermuda triangle perspective, that if things aren't going well and if church planting requires sacrifice and brings difficulty that perhaps the best solution is to forget the dream.

The Bermuda Triangle

That Bermuda triangle is right where the enemy wants you. The enemy uses the triangulation of **fear, doubt**, and **resentment** to suck the life right out of a planter's wife. Satan knows that if he can hit us from all three sides, the chances of us whispering such thoughts of giving up to our husbands are very high. This road of church planting is hard!

When we are discouraged, weary and tired we are vulnerable to this very destructive pattern. Tears flow as I write this because I have been there many times. There are times I feel like the church plant is a never ending leech that asks more and more of me, no matter how much I give. This feeling is compounded even more when I have prayed and asked God for certain things and yet there is silence, or when the continual worry and fear of finances weighs on us. In these very crucial moments, I can either be used of God to speak life, faith and encouragement to my husband, or I can drag him down into that Bermuda triangle of death with me. Never underestimate the power your words have on your husband.

El Roi - The God Who Sees You

I realize this chapter is very heavy and it is not my intention to condemn or judge anyone. I hope I have shared enough of my struggle with this very issue of faith and trust in God to let you know that it is a very real issue for me. It has crippled me, debilitated me, and continues to be a thorn in my side. I know that God is using this journey to refine me and to teach me that *He* is all I need. God made us the way we are and He is aware of our needs. He knows you have need for stability and security. He is pleased with your faith in Him and your hard work. He knows, my friend that you get weary and need some magic along the way to keep going. God sees **YOU**.

Church planting requires more of you, than you ever thought possible. It is not easy, nor is it a comfortable way to live, but are we just about being comfortable or are we about living a life passionate for the cause of Christ?

Obeying the call to plant a church requires hard work, faith in God and for us to stick with it even when we want to quit. You, my friend play a crucial role in the plan God has set out for the city He has called you and your husband to reach. The Lord has used women to accomplish great things for Him and wants to use you as well!

What I am learning is that I can wholeheartedly trust Him. I can put my faith in Him and even in the times I hear nothing but silence, God works to accomplish amazing things. Sometimes, it is in His silence that He is doing the most work.

There is no magic formula and there is no pixie dust, but there is a God who is mindful of you and sees you. A few months ago I re-read the story of Hagar. It is one I have read countless times, but God used this story on a particular day to speak to me in a very real and powerful way. Genesis 16:1-15, tells the story of Hagar, Sarah and Abraham who were engaged in quite the love triangle. Sarah who could not conceive a child gave her maidservant Hagar over to her husband, Abraham. Sarah became jealous of Hagar once she was pregnant, so she mistreated her. Verse 6 of Genesis, chapter 16 tells us that Hagar fled from Sarah into a spring near the desert. Hagar was full of anguish and fear, but an angel of the Lord came to Hagar and told her to return to Sarah and submit to her.

I don't know about you, but I do not think I would have been happy about this command. I mean let's be real. Sarah had the grand idea to give Hagar to her husband in order to conceive a child, then she mistreats her, Hagar flees and God tells her to return to the situation and submit?

After the command was given to Hagar to submit to Sarah, then the promise followed that God would make her son Ishmael into a great nation. Talk about some pixie dust! Hagar then addressed God in a powerful way as "El-Roi," which means, *The God Who Sees Me.*" In Genesis 16:13, she says, "You are the God who sees me, I have now seen the One who see me." (NIV)

Maybe you feel the anguish Hagar did and feel abandoned by God. Perhaps you are crying in the desert and your faith has shriveled up. Rest assured that where there is a desert, there is also a spring present to provide living water for your soul. God stands ready to provide that living water and fill your tank with faith, yet we cannot forget the first command given to Hagar. The angel told her to *return* to her situation and *submit.*

Another word for submit is surrender. I don't know about you but I like to be in control and I do not like to relinquish control to someone else. Submission to God is key to living a victorious, faith filled life. Without surrender to God, we will never see the promise of a harvest. The God who asks for our total and complete submission to Him and His process also provides the promise to provide, restore and bless your hard work.

Just A Little Pixie Dust

Today "El-Roi" wants you to know, He sees *you.*

He sees your obedience, your sacrifice, and your hard work. He is also mindful of your need for security and stability. God has called you as a church planter's wife to do amazing things for Him. Along the way, He is also using the journey of church planting to refine you and teach you more about Him.

My prayer for us as planter wives is that we learn to completely rely on our Father, and realize that He is truly all we need. Coming to this kind of dependence on God is not easy and requires complete surrender and submission to Him. The promise at the end of obedience is incredible. You and I are not alone and when we are weary; my challenge is that we look for that spring in the desert and hold on to a God who will never let us go.

Let us not become weary in doing good because at the proper time, we will reap a harvest if we do not give up. With faith, hard work and a little *Divine* pixie dust, your diligence and perseverance will pay off.

Part IV

Things That Make You Go Hmmmm

> He who finds a wife finds
> what is good
> and receives favor from
> the LORD.
> Proverbs 18:22

CHAPTER 12

What Every Planter Wishes His Wife Knew

Written by Church Planter – Jon Hamp

A Mile in His Shoes

Everyone has imagined what it would be like to walk a mile in someone else's shoes. Live their lives for a day. Feel what they feel. Know what they know. That would be fun, wouldn't it? It would be interesting to see the world through someone else's eyes— even if just for a while.

Even more common than the desire to understand others though, is our desire for people to see the world through *our eyes*. Walk a mile in *our shoes*. To see the world the way *we see it*. This, of course, stems from our own desire to be understood. After all, who doesn't long to be understood? Naturally, we especially want to be understood by our spouse.

Your husband is no different; he wants you to understand him. However, nothing complicates understanding you husband more than when he is a church planter.

Earlier in the book, Angie compares church planting to "riding a roller coaster" and that is an apt comparison for many reasons. The experience evokes the gamut of emotions: fear, excitement, exhilaration, anticipation, and relief. Oh, and let's not forget about physical effects like exhaustion, adrenaline rush, and of course, nausea, and vomiting. I digress. My point is this: for your husband, the answer to the question "how are you?" can change on a dime, and often does so many times within the same 24-hour period, especially, if you ask on a Sunday. We men are not as in-tune with our feelings and emotions to as our wives to begin with, so conveying to someone else what is going on inside us can be nearly impossible.

What I have attempted to do in this chapter is to provide a glimpse of three dynamics that often impact a planter's marriage. I have also tried to share some of the motivation behind the strange behaviors we planters are likely to undertake in the course of planting a church. They are principles that, though we may not be able to articulate them to you, we are screaming from the inside, and living out through our actions and decisions. Not all of these principles will apply to every planter or planter's marriage, but along the journey most will experience at least some of these dynamics. This is your chance to walk a mile in your husband's shoes.

Principle One: He Cannot Do This Alone.

I realize you already know this. At least you think you do. Ostensibly, you understand that your husband needs your support, your help, and your presence. You know that ministry is not a one-sided calling in a marriage and that it will always involve both of you. Angie has already covered this ground quite well, so I am not going to re-open that discussion.

What I want you to do is *feel* the effects of what you already know. Your husband may never say it. He may never say it in a way that resonates with you, but deep inside he is trying to tell you "I need you" and he does. More than you know.

Church planting is scary for anyone. Often the older a person gets, the less likely they are to undertake planting a church. As a result, many church planters are younger and consequently their marriages are newer. The concepts of co-ownership and cooperation on a project are many times still points of learning in young marriages, but church planting requires a great deal of both. That can place a heavy strain on new marriages and create opportunities for disharmony that might not otherwise exist.

As a man who has decided to plant a church, your husband has already proven that he is fiercely independent, motivated, entrepreneurial, and strong. Not when it comes to you however. Your husband *needs you* more than anything else. He needs you by his side at fundraisers, in public, at launch services, and at small groups. He needs you behind him when the new church faces hardship, conflict, budget deficits, and crises. He needs you to go before him in prayer and lift him up daily to God. He also needs you to have his back when people turn against him, leave the church, or gossip about him—even (or particularly) when he is wrong. Your husband *needs* you in a very big way.

I know what you may be thinking, *"But this is his calling, not mine"* and, you are mostly right, but only mostly. He cannot be expected to do this without you any more than you should be expected to raise your children without him. Can it be done? Sure. Can it be done as well as if the two of you cooperate to do it together? No. The best and most successful church plants are those that have solid husband and wife teams. This does not mean you need to do everything, or even almost everything in the new church. What it does mean, is that your husband, who *needs* you, has you— beside him, behind him, and before him.

I know that for me my wife is a safety blanket in just about every setting. Even if she is not playing an active role in the execution of a particular event, just her being there is a stabilizing force for me. She lends an air of refinement and grace to any function and is a true partner in every sense of the word. I could not do this without her. I need her, and our church needs her. I thank God that she is who she is—our church would not be where it is today without her.

Principle Two: The Mathematics of Feedback

I have a simple axiom that I apply to feedback: it is human nature to double, or even triple, the importance of negative feedback received from others. It is also human nature to minimize the importance of positive feedback received and to think of reasons that it may not be entirely accurate. When the feedback is from your spouse, the mathematics become even more significant.

Not too long ago, I delivered a message on a Sunday morning that was, admittedly, not my best. Later that same day, at lunch, our worship leader indicated to me that he thought my delivery was weak and dispassionate. That was hard to take, but palatable. I asked him to expound on his statement, and he did, at some length in fact. I validated his statements, asked questions, agreed where I could, and in general, took his feedback quite well.

After lunch, when we got in the car, I asked Angie what she thought about my message, and she replied simply: *"It was good, but you didn't seem like yourself today."* That was certainly a softer way to say things in comparison to how my worship leader had said them, but it hit me like a ton of bricks. *"Wow, I didn't realize I was so bad"* I responded sharply. She never said I was bad. She said that I wasn't myself, which I already knew was true—but boy did it hurt coming from her.

I could give you real-life example after real-life example of how much more meaningful and "weighty" my wife's feedback is compared to anyone else's. I have learned that there is a different mathematical formula applied to feedback from my wife. In general, I tend to multiply negative feedback by 10, and divide positive feedback by at least two. The reasons are quite simple.

First, let's look at positive feedback. Angie is my wife. If she didn't think I was incredible, amazing, handsome, sexy, thoughtful, introspective, deep, theologically sound, and an excellent communicator, she never would have married me to begin with. So when she tells me *"You did a great job today!"* I translate it as: *"Hey you*

lived up to what I already knew you were capable of today."
No credit earned, just what was expected. At least, just
what was--in my mind. So any positive feedback from
her will be divided by at least a factor of two.

Negative feedback though is a different story. Again,
Angie is my wife right? So obviously she loves me, and
thinks I am the most powerful communicator to ever
hold a microphone and stand in front of a church and
preach the word. Clearly she knows what I am capable
of and how hard I work to make every week a "home-
run." She also understands how much her input means
to me, and that, aside from God himself, no one's feedback means more. (She does understand that, right?) So
for her to give me any negative feedback (which she
knows will crush me) things must be really, really bad.
Her negative feedback will be multiplied by at least 10.

This does not mean you cannot and should not give
your husband honest feedback. You should however,
think long and hard about what you are saying and how
best you should say it. He gives his time, energy, and
efforts to others in ministry, but you hold his heart and
his spirit. Be careful that you do not inadvertently crush
it by being too critical. Also, do not be afraid to heap on
the compliments. Validate all of the positive things he is
doing and how hard he works and how much people
(and you specifically) appreciate his efforts. You have to
say it more than you think before he will hear it— and he
needs to hear it.

Principle Three: The Dragon Slayer Principle

Men are hunters. We stalk our prey, waiting until the
ideal moment before we strike, and when we do, we aim
for the kill. We play to win. When we bring down the

beast, we are really saying, *"I love you, and I did this for you."* Your husband will pour himself into the new church. He will work tirelessly. He will spend more time away from his family than ever before, and hardly notice. He will spend funds from your personal finances for the church plant without thinking twice. He will ask you to sacrifice time, wealth, convenience, and sleep, to help make the church plant a success. He is stalking the prey. He is saying, *"I love you."* I know it does not seem that way, but he is. Trust me.

Your husband is wired in a different way than you are. When the two of you joined hands, looked into each other's eyes and said, *"Okay, let's plant a church together"* he heard you say, *"Go get 'em big boy— slay the dragon!"* In his heart, he wants to throw the carcass of a beast on the table with a barbaric grunt and have you look approvingly at him and say, "That's my man, the dragon-slayer."

As men we need that challenge, and we need that approval. Sometimes though, our pursuit of it will make it seem like we have traded our family and marriage for a dream. In real life, we know that happens all of the time, but recognizing the difference between selling out and digging in is not always easy.

It is important for you to remember that, as with all ministries, church planting has its seasons of busyness and rest. The few months before the launch of a new church and the few months after launch will require more of your husband than the early stages of forming a launch-team, or the formative time after the first full year. Some seasons will require more understanding on your part of your husband's stress load, work-habits, and time management than others. Just know that up front.

However, your husband needs you to be the voice of reason—even during the unavoidable "sprint moments" in ministry. Do not be afraid to champion your family, your marriage, and his wise use of time during seasons of particular strain. Just be careful not to become nagging. This is where *how* say things becomes even more important than *what* you say. Remember, he's trying to prove he loves you by making this church plant successful. Your husband is trying to validate your love and admiration for him by slaying the dragon. His intent has never been to get out of spending time together. He is working for a bigger goal than just today, bigger than just this moment, and sometimes his focus will become too narrow.

Angie has learned to make non-threatening statements like *"I'd love to spend some time alone with you soon"* to remind me of the importance of our marriage, or *"The boys were telling me today how much they love you, and that they haven't gotten to see you much this week"* to remind me to make our family a priority. This way of communicating expresses a desire to share life with me without being critical. It points to the needs of my family, not to my faults. Yes, the faults are real, but often they are the by-products of a desire to succeed. Angie has become skilled at gently reminding me that success in my family and marriage is just as important (and even more rewarding) than success in the church plant without making me feel criticized or threatened.

Final Thoughts

As a planter's wife you have a unique opportunity to partner with your husband in a way that most wives of professionals never will. For other women, it is "his job" and "his work" and "his success." Sometimes, you will long for that separation, but when you do, remember that the women who have that separation are probably looking at you wishing they had an opportunity to partner with their husband as closely as you do.

Speaking from the role of a church planter whose wife is a "full-partner" I can tell you, I love every minute of it, and I could never do this without her. Embrace your joint calling and enjoy the journey with your husband— he will be forever thankful to you for it.

> Where there is no coun-
> sel, the people fall; but in
> the multitude of counse-
> lors there is safety."
> Proverbs 11:14

CHAPTER 13

I Wish I Would Have Known That
Real Life Advice from Church Planter's Wives

The old saying, "hindsight is 20/20" is used when a person reflects back on how they might have done things differently. Upon reflection of most things we do in life, the information we gained through trial and error, hardship and failure could have served us well had we had it before beginning the journey. The same concept holds true in church planting. This chapter is replete with knowledge and wisdom from other church planter's wives who have walked the road, and desire to share their nuggets of advice with other planter wives. The hope is that as you read the advice from other planter wives, your vision will be clearer as you walk the road of church planting.

On Marriage

Mary Beth Bradshaw – Wife of Church Planting Director – Michigan

#1- Have lots of SEX! It can be the one connection you have when everything else is haywire. It brings you back together, and is a very important stress reliever for your driven man. Carve out time whenever you can get it; when kids go to school a quick lunch... or rendezvous at home.

It is also important to take vacations without the kids. I always felt VERY guilty doing this at first. My husband planned vacations, and said "we are going.' Once I got to our destination it was WONDERFUL.

Chasity Ross – Brighton Colorado

A lot of times we didn't have balance. It seemed between work and ministry, sometimes the kids came last or for that matter my husband and I came last. We almost functioned as roommates. When the kids go to bed, Tony and I spend time together, watch movie, play a game, talk, whatever...Tony made an announcement to the church that this was his day off and is our family day, and not to call him or email him because he will not respond, pick up the phone, or read email. If it was a true emergency he encouraged people to contact someone on the leadership team. We committed to each other to not talk about the church or ministry at all on family day, so that we would have a true family day, and day off for my husband.

Renee Exley – Life Church - Midlothian, Texas

Jason and I go on dates quite often. I'm a strong believer in putting my boys to bed by 8:00 p.m. That way we have time to catch up or just to sit in quiet together. It is all about staying sane!

Bonnie Rolf – Freedom Church - McKinney, Texas

We have one day a week off together & then Jason takes another day of just filling up, and resting. I also try to take a day where I do the same but I'm not as balanced as Jase, and often let things and people fill my time often, but I am getting better. We have shared with our church that on those days they can connect with other leaders or each other there is an emergency, and that is the church being based on the saints not the pastor.

Amber Woller – Corner Church – Minneapolis, MN

Before we planted a church, my husband had been a youth pastor, and I was an elementary teacher. The demands on my time were overwhelming, especially with two little girls. There were many reasons why I decided to stop teaching, but a major factor was the state of my marriage. Our marriage was falling apart although it was not because I was overworked. As we worked to repair it, we realized that our ministry would be more effective if done together. Although it has been tough financially, we committed to not being bi-vocational. We knew the demands of bi-vocational work would cause either our family/ marriage or our ministry to suffer.

D.F. –Texas

In terms of marriage, get away together....often! You

have to step away from it...and step away from it a lot. My parents go somewhere every quarter...and they've been at their church for 21 years. You need to get away for staying power.

On Family

Chasity Ross – Brighton Colorado

We set up a family night and the kids love it and look forward to it. We do things like watch movies, make popcorn, play board games, or if we were lucky and had some gift cards we save them for family night and go out.

Renee Exley – Life Church - Midlothian, Texas

There have been so many family nights that include doing stuff for the church ex. Cleaning the church, the Costco run, all the little stuff like that, but we tend to add something fun in there too. Basically, we as a family are always together.

Julie Strait – Pathway Church – Longview, Texas

My husband, Marty grew up in a pastor's home and I grew up in a family where my dad was a work-a-holic, so we both purposed in our family from the beginning that our family would not be neglected for the sake of the church. Fortunately I have been able to stay at home with the kids and I home schooled until January of this year. So, that gave me a lot of time with the kids. Marty (although he was working 7 days a week for a while) is the kid's coach for basketball, baseball, etc, and he is always at special events. We have "special daddy days" like going to the zoo. Our kids are still at the ages that they think it is cool to hang out with us, so we try to do fun things with them like bowling or putt-putt a couple of times a month.

Allison Crum – High Calling Church – Eastpoint, FL

We always spend our evenings together as a family, and we, too, adhere to bedtime for our children. We try to schedule family outings (with Dad) at least every two months.

D. F. – Texas

We never told our kids if anything negative was going on in the church. I didn't want my kids to walk away with anything they could harbor bitterness about. As a pastor's kid myself, I think this is SO important. My parents never let me in on anything negative that went on. I walked away from my PK experience with a very positive outlook and I want my kids to do the same. But while I'm on that, it was important to us that we never put extra pressure on our children because they were the pastor's kids. We never mentioned it and usually, neither did anyone else. But if they had, we would have said something. **PROTECT YOUR KIDS!**

Cherri Pike – Wife of Assemblies of God Church Planting Director

My primary focus when my kids were home was **ALWAYS** my children. Even though I worked, it was never a career; it was just to help make ends meet. My logic was that people would have lots of pastor's wives during their lifetime but my children only would have one mom.

Taking Care of Yourself

Rachael Scott – Family Room Church – Hardwick, GA

I am most productive in the evenings. I am not a morning person at all. My husband takes our two children oldest to school so that I can rest or sleep in a little longer, and get some Jesus time. Granted, there are some days I have to take them or need to be up but most of the time I stay home in the morning. I also make sure I'm in the Word. Even if it's while I'm cooking I will have it playing on an app on my Iphone. Worship music is a must to rejuvenate my spirit. Other things that some may think are no big deal are huge to me... A simple pedicure, a hair wash (not even a cut just a wash), a coffee from Starbucks, and maybe an hour alone at Barnes & Noble.

D.F. – Texas

The gym was a real release for Randy and his stress. It was a MUST! We have to take care of our physical bodies. On the spiritual side, the statistics are alarming at how many pastors do not have a personal prayer time and time in the word every day. For many pastors they read just enough to preach a sermon. This cannot be the case! Spending time with our God is more important than anything else we can do to take care of ourselves. He is our sustainer.

Relationships

Rachael Scott – Family Room Church – Hardwick, GA

Yes!Yes!Yes! Honestly, without such relationships I would have quit, and given in. Being intentional about finding others in the same spot or farther down the road is just as important as feeding my soul. The ladies I have met thru blogging, facebook, or other women in ministry motivate me, challenge my thinking, and embrace me from thousands of miles away.

D.F. – Texas

This is the hardest one in my opinion. We learned it in Bible College. Be friends with everyone, and best friends with no one. It is true. It is lonely, but it is true. We found that so many people wanted to be best friends with the pastor. But the pastors had a best friend...each other! We learned that when you are their pastor, you will always be seen differently. You may as well just accept it. You don't get to say everything you think, or do anything you want to do. You must always consider those around you, but truly, it should be this way for every Christian. Christians just don't like that to apply to them the way they want it to apply to their pastors. The loneliness of Pastoring is something no one could have prepared us for. There could be countless books written on this subject alone. We found that many pastors were not being real or honest when in "ministerial meeting" type settings. It always felt a bit more like a competition than it did fellowship. One pastor says what his church did for missions and another one ups him. Then a pastor would say how many they had on Sunday, and another pastor would one up him. No one ever said, "hey, I am lonely, I need a friend...this is hard, I'm doing my best, but things aren't great!" very few are ever this honest. And when they are, it's because they are at their breaking point.

Mary Beth Bradshaw – Wife of Church Planting Director – Michigan

I had some pastor's wives I called when I needed them, and I did. There were also some in our community that I had relationship with. I also had prayer warriors in the church. I would never hesitate to ask them to pray, and sometimes I would share details; other times I did not. They never pushed for those intimate things. IF they would have I would not have trusted them like I did. They were safe.

On Balance

Chasity Ross – Brighton Colorado

We had to seriously lay down some boundaries as far as ministry was concerned. Finding balance, especially when it comes to church planting is quite the challenge; our biggest ministry is our children and each other, then the church. This balance is hard when in church planting, it's all you think about and you both carry so much burden for people, details of the church, pressures, and stress.

Renee Exley – Life Church - Midlothian, Texas

We both grew up in a ministers home so we learned

how important it is to keep things balanced. There are times it gets uneven, but we have learned to step back and take a break.

Bonnie Rolf – Freedom Church - McKinney, Texas

We have what we call **"no church zone"** if one of us or both of us is feeling over done by church stuff we call a **no church zone** and we don't discuss church. It's been amazing but hard. We have also scheduled non negotiable times, such as working out & our quiet time. That has helped.

Julie Strait – Pathway Church – Longview, Texas

I wanted to have a healthy family and a healthy church and I knew that I had the ability to function in all of the roles. What I didn't know was I didn't have the capability to be more than one person. LOL! I have learned to trust God in that we do not have to have everything in our church at this season for it to be what God wants it to be right now. And, it's okay for me to take some time for myself away from my kids. In fact, it is absolutely necessary for me to let a few things go.

Amber Woller – Corner Church – Minneapolis, MN

I try to remember something my mom once said, *"We make time for what's important."* Whenever I feel like I don't have enough time, I ask myself, *"What is important?"* Instead of saying, *"I don't have the time for something,"* I realize that I am choosing not to take the time for it. Either it isn't important to me, or I am letting unimportant things take over.

Mary Beth Bradshaw – Wife of Church Planting Director – Michigan

Balance. That is a crazy word in ministry. I think one way to be balanced is to be flexible. Ministry can be so unpredictable. As much as we guarded our off day... and planned family nights and outing... (Extremely VITAL AREAS TO BE INTENTIONAL ABOUT) there were times when life happened. People die, have crisis, get sick, etc. During those situations, I had to be flexible. Some days we rearranged, or changed our day off; however being stressed out about it would only heighten the anxiety and frustration my husband felt about having to leave. He didn't WANT to have to go and leave us but it is his (our) calling. My willingness to be flexible at these times made it easier for Him to do ministry and for my kids to roll with it and not resent ministry.

Our Best Advice

Allison Crum – High Calling Church – Eastpoint, FL

My best advice is to be patient! I've tried reading books about being a help meet, and I've attended marriage classes. However, all I can say now is pray and be patient (with your husband and children). During this period of my life, I find myself increasingly overwhelmed. The house is dirty, the homework isn't finished, the uniforms aren't washed, the baby has a dirty diaper, I have an evaluation at work, my husband is never home, etc! All I know to do is STOP and pray. So, that's what I do on good days. During other times, I survive. I try always to look on the bright side and take pleasure in the blessings God has given me-a loving husband, healthy children, and a growing church. It may sounds cliché, but it's true.

Amber Woller – Corner Church – Minneapolis, MN

1) Figure out your role. What do you feel comfortable with? If you work full-time outside the home, your role will be different than someone who works full-time, church planting. Each wife's role is different, which is perfectly fine as long as you and your husband are in agreement about what is right for you. It doesn't matter what other wives do or what a congregation expects as long as you are doing what God wants.
2) You are the best advocate for you and your family. Be willing to set boundaries and explain expectations. Be willing to say no and to ask for what is right. There is a point where people will abuse your sacrifices, and we must be willing to advocate for ourselves and our families.
3) Be willing to seek friendships and even professional help outside of the church. Our time is stretched so thinly, but having someone to whom we can confide our worries and stresses can save our sanity as well as our marriage.
4) Keep track of the times God provided and did amazing things in your church planting journey. Recall those moments during the difficult days.

5) Remember that your success may not look like someone else's success, but that doesn't mean it is any less.

Kay Gowins – Two Time Church Planter's Wife

After planting two churches, one successful and one not so much, "one" of the pieces of advice I would like to share, happens at the onset. Make certain that the teams you form are people that you have some history with, that you know WELL, that share your vision, your approach, your methods and your theology. Unity is essential.

Rachael Scott – Family Room Church – Hardwick, GA

You and Jesus need to be number one; plain and simple. If the two of you aren't okay nothing else will be. If you can't find time for the one who is going to give you all the Grace to get thru this season in your life, then you need to turn around and say forget it right now.

Your marriage is a priority over your church, and your children. Yes your children and your church need you, however your spouse NEEDS you more, and you need him. He was there first before the kids, and when they move on he will be the one with you; this relationship needs to be maintained! Involve your children and talk it up. If you talk down about the problems so will they.

Remember Ephesians 5:2msg. His love was not cautious but extravagant. He didn't love in order to get something from us but to give everything of himself to us. Love like that.

D.F. - Texas

Hold people loosely. Not everyone will be with you forever. No matter how much it may seem like they will be and no matter how much you may want them to be. When we first planted our church, we were told that some people are scaffolding and some people are bricks. In other words, some people are there to help you build, but they are temporary. While other people are there permanently, they will always be there, and we learned that it's nearly impossible to identify who is in what group.

Beth Edwards – Rural Church Planting – Wyoming

I guess some advice might be to let the rural people be themselves and allow them to worship how they are comfortable. A lot of rural folks are conservative and don't really get into the jumping and shouting and running around. That doesn't mean they're not worshipping and in touch with God. They just have a different method of expressing themselves. And frequently, what works for bigger churches, won't work for a rural community. And sometimes, it might. It's a lot of trying things and seeing what works. Listen to the people of that area - they are pretty aware of what will fly and what won't. Accept all the talents that they (the church) have and then see if they will stretch a bit to help the church to grow. Some will and some will not. Be relaxed - it's ok to wear jeans to church. Be flexible as well.

Mary Beth Bradshaw – Wife of Church Planting Director – Michigan

BE WHO YOU ARE! Do not feel you have to 'measure up' to anyone else but who GOD has called you to be. Your call is unique to you. How you walk that out is something HE will empower you to do in an individual way. Don't compare yourself to other wives, church plants, their successes, growth, style, etc. Know the culture of your community and who GOD has called you to reach as a church and as a believer... not just as the pastor's wife. This will energize you.

Just One More Tidbit

I hope you enjoyed reading real life advice from other church planter's wives. These women are in the trenches of church planting and have the war wounds to prove it. They are also wise beyond their years and have a heart for church planter wives just like you! You are not alone in your journey. There are fellow women who have also answered the call and serve with you on the journey of church planting. Rest assured you are lifted up in prayer on a regular basis, so stand firm and embrace the journey.

Part V

Last But Not Least

> Sometimes you put up
> walls not to keep people
> out, but to see who cares
> enough to
> break them down.
> ~Jeanette Winterson~

CHAPTER 14

The Importance of Relationships
Ways to Connect With Other Planter Wives

Pastors and their wives are some of the worst at connecting in relationships. We do a fantastic job of connecting with people in our church and preach about how crucial relationships are, but when it comes to our own lives we often neglect this in our own lives. Many women shy away from relationships with other pastors wives and yet this can be our greatest source of encouragement and support. The bottom line is that as a planter wife you need to be in relationship with other planter wives. There is such power and comfort in spending time with someone who *gets it*, and can help share the burdens you deal with on a daily basis. It is also important for you to seek to be a source of encouragement to other planter wives. There is strength in numbers and having relationships you can draw from will serve you well in times of hardship and stress. Being in relationship with other planter wives may not have been something you have considered so far, but I promise you that these relationships will be ones that you will cherish and hold dear. So, what are some ways you can find other planter wives to share the journey of church planting with?

Look Around You

Church planting has become very popular and it seems that new churches are springing up everywhere. Praise God! Be on the lookout in the town you live in for new churches. Rather than view a new church as competition, seek out the wife of the church planter, and ask her to coffee. This may seem forward and outside of your comfort zone, but I guarantee you she will appreciate your efforts to connect.

If you are connected with a particular denomination, call or email your leadership and ask them to provide you with information of church planters and their wives. This might require some effort on your part, but it will be worth it. When you see a new sign for a new church go up, take that as your sign to connect with that planter wife.

The Facebook Connection

Facebook is a wonderful tool for communicating and connecting with other planter wives. Use this tool to become friends with other planter wives. Watch their status updates and if there is a particular need they express take that as your opportunity to send them an encouraging message and to pray for them. What goes around comes around, and rest assured that as you seek to encourage other planter wives through facebook, you will also receive that same encouragement back when you have difficult days.

Another way to connect via facebook with other planter wives is to join a facebook group. There are numerous facebook groups out there already, so search for one and join a group. You can also create your own facebook group where you can post questions or allow women to post prayer requests and ideas they are implementing in their church plants.

The Hype with Skype

Many church planting organizations provide training events for their planters. Church planters and their spouses attend these events and form connections but many of them live in different parts of the country. Skype is a valuable tool that allows you to remain connected with other planter wives you meet at training events and conferences. It is a simple to set up on your computer and since most laptops have cameras built in, all that you need is a set of headphones and you are ready to go.

I meet with a group of women who live all over the country once a month via skype. We discuss different topics, swap ideas, laugh with one another and pray with each other. I look forward to our monthly meeting and am so grateful for these relationships. Don't let the miles keep you apart, but instead implement technology to build and cultivate relationships with other planter wives.

cpwives.com

Cpwives.com is a website that provides resources, encouragement and pathways of connection for church planter wives. This website provides articles relating to issues that impact planter wives. In addition the website has links to blogs of other church planter wives that enjoy connecting with planter wives. cpwives.com also has church planter wives from across the country that have availed themselves to mentor, coach and talk to planter wives. You simply have to go on the website, click on the region where you live and there are names and email addresses of other planter wives who would be honored to connect with you.

There are also skype groups that happen during different days and times of the week where you can join and discuss relevant topics with other planter wives. This website is a wonderful tool that provides pathways for relationships with other planter wives. It is a place where you will find encouragement, interesting articles and other women you can connect with, no matter where you live.

You Need Relationship

You may have been hesitant up to this point to connect with other planter wives. Perhaps the fear of being vulnerable or a sense of competition has kept you from pursuing relationships with other church planter wives. I encourage you lay all of that aside and step out. You may have to extend your hand of friendship to another planter wife, but it will be well worth it.

There have been days where I felt so hopeless and weary, I thought I was losing my mind until one of my soul sisters who was either led by the Holy Spirit, or I called stood ready to encourage me, cheerlead me and pray with me. I honestly do not know how I would have made it through many darks days if it had not been for my church planting sisters. Don't make the mistake of being a lone ranger in this journey of church planting. We all need relationship and I promise you, you will receive blessing and encouragement from your relationships with other planter wives and will be used to as a blessing and source of encouragement.

> The bottom line is:
> YOU ROCK!
>
> ~Angie Hamp~

CHAPTER 15

Final Thoughts

Thank you for taking time to read my *confessions*. The purpose of this book was to provide a living room where you could take time to sit, read and reflect on being a church planter's wife. I hope that throughout the book the voice of God spoke to you and that His presence was near to you. I pray you found some freedom from guilt and loneliness, and discovered more about you and what God has for you.

As church planter wives we are a unique breed of women. We are strong, dedicated and rise to the challenges church planting brings our way. We have dignity, grace and poise. We are talented, beautiful, gracious and kind. God views us this way and I hope that you caught just a glimpse of how our Father sees you. Nothing and no one compares to you.

My prayer is that as you continue on this road of church planting, you find confidence in yourself, your abilities and your unique calling. Your role is not an easy one, but God will give you what you need, when you need it. No matter the situation or difficulty, you have the ability to rise up and meet the challenge. There is a world out there that needs women who will stand up for their, *such a time as this*, and He has chosen us as a church planter's wives for such a purpose.

We may not be able to grasp the far-reach of what we do week in and week out, until eternity, but know this; people will stand in heaven because of you. God has called you and equipped you to reach people that may not otherwise be reached. No matter your background, race, socio-economic status, labels, past, you are a daughter of the Most High King. He sees you and He is pleased with you. WHAT YOU DO MATTERS!

To find out more about Angie Hamp and her ministry to church planter's wives please visit: confessionsofachurchplanterswife.com.

About   The   Author:

Angie Hamp is a wife, mother, retreat speaker, College Faculty, a Licensed Professional Counselor and – **church planter's wife**. Angie and her husband Jon have been married for 16 years and have two boys; Noah is 12 and Caleb is 10.

Jon and Angie have a long history of church planting. They served at a church plant in Riverton, Utah as Associate Pastors for four years and then moved to Colorado Springs, Colorado to be Associate Pastors at a church plant, where they served for another four years. In September 2009, Jon and Angie launched Discovery Church in Parker, Colorado (South Denver) as Lead Pastors. The church is healthy and vibrant, and is in a community where less than 12% of the population, attend church. They desire to plant churches all over the Denver area. They have developed a church-planter-in-residence program to recruit, train, and release church planters to start new churches.

Angie has a burden for church planter's wives and spends several hours a week talking with planter wives. Her desire is to minister to planter wives and convey to them that *what they do matters.*

In her spare time, Angie enjoys running, dancing, writing, football, drinking coffee, listening to very loud, hard rock music, and hanging out in the Colorado Mountains with her husband and children.

8795332R0

Made in the USA
Charleston, SC
15 July 2011